101 Recipes for Gluten-Free Microwave Mug Cakes:

Healthier Single-Serving Snacks in Less Than 10 Minutes

101 Recipes for Gluten-Free Microwave Mug Cakes:

Healthier Single-Serving Snacks in Less Than 10 Minutes

Stacey J. Miller

****

BPT Press
P. O. Box 834
Randolph, MA 02368-0834

Book cover by Kristine Hanson
Edited by Ruth Loetterle
Interior design by Amy Ruth Seigal
Page composition by Peter Martin

To my mom who passed along to me her love for homemade, simple cooking. This book happened only because of her unwavering faith in me and her belief that, if things don't go right in the kitchen, they won't go right anywhere.

ABOUT THE AUTHOR

Stacey J. Miller learned at a very young age that, on days when nothing else goes right, she can always make herself feel better by cooking an easy meal or baking a quick dessert. When she's not in the kitchen, she's indulging in her day job. A book promotion specialist, Stacey founded S. J. Miller Communications. She is based in Randolph, Massachusetts and is the author of *101 Recipes for Microwave Mug Cakes: Single-Serving Snacks in Less Than 10 Minutes* (BPT Press).

Visit *101 Recipes for Gluten-Free Microwave Mug Cakes* online: www.microwavemugcakes.com

CONTENTS

ACKNOWLEDGEMENTS

Who knew that "gluten-free" baking meant that everything I'd ever learned about baking would have to be re-thought, re-conceptualized, and re-mastered? I've been baking, cooking, and just generally making messes in the kitchen since I was old enough to stand on a chair to stir the chocolate pudding. But gluten-free baking provided me with an opportunity to learn it all over again, and who could have imagined the results would be so satisfying and exciting?

No one creates a cookbook alone.

Thanks, mom, for sharing with me your love for playing, exploring, and learning in the kitchen, and for giving me the confidence to do it, whatever it takes, and however many failures (which are just steppingstones on the path to success) get tossed into the trash. How many mothers, besides you, would have eaten that mess that was supposed to be lentil soup when I was about 14 years old, and I had forgotten to stir it for about two hours? None, and that's why you're you, and that's why you're the greatest. You proved it all over again when I traded in the tried-and-true ingredients for the unknown, gluten-free possibilities. And thanks, dad, for once again coming through as a front-line beta microwave mug cakes tester. Your cast-iron stomach has proved invaluable time and time again.

Amy, your enthusiasm and support mean everything in the world to me. Without you, there would be no microwave mug cake books. Someday, we'll explore New York together the right way (and, by that, I mean that one of us will bring along a GPS!). We might even discover there's more to see there in the City than the Empire State Building (with its stirring view of that sewage treatment plant – and I'm so glad you snapped that particular picture!).

Scott, you finally got to see what the microwave mug cake craze is all about. It was truly an honor to name the microwave mug cake you helped create after my favorite nephew. (Jackie: I really wanted to name that microwave mug cake after you, too … but Scott's decision was final, I'm afraid. Next time.)

Alyssa, your singing provided the soundtrack to my testing sessions when I turned the kitchen into the gluten-free microwave mug cake lab. And, Jessica, your mathematic and scientific mind kept me glued to my measuring spoons, recipe after recipe.

Maria and John, you were right. People shouldn't work 24/7/365 (and you both need to be reminded of that, too!). Thank you for getting me out of the kitchen for some of the best times ever, and thank you for being my true siblings of the heart.

Speaking of siblings of the heart, thanks to the Debs (both of you!), Sue, Kris, Martha, Kim (Teabag), Other Kim, Vikki, Val, Marilyn, Nancy, Doreen, Jane, Diane, Charlene, Gail, Norma, Malinda, Sasha, Nancy, Betty, Cindy, and Lia – and all the cat lovers of MMT and beyond.

And, of course, thanks are due to my biological sister, Nancy, too. Thank you for sharing some of my best genes, Nancy, and thank you for lending your support to my microwave mug cake baking adventure. It means a lot to me.

Thank you, Susan and Darlene, for being my literary touchstones. And to Debra … you are my role model, and you've demonstrated to me how to do it with style (beginning with the self-published version of *The Fine Art of Small Talk*) for years. I wouldn't have dared to start on this path if you hadn't already blazed the trail, my friend.

And Barbara, I'm still grateful to you for being the first to send me that wonderful recipe for baking a chocolate mug cake in the microwave. And, Pat, my thanks still go out to you for posting a link to that chocolate mug cake recipe on your Facebook account at exactly the right time. You both helped line up the stars for me.

To readers everywhere who lobbied for gluten-free, healthier microwave mug cake recipes – and to everyone who shared tips and ideas for making gluten-free and healthier versions of microwave mug cakes taste even better than the originals – my sincere thanks.

Finally, Steve, Ruth, Noah, and Audrey: you willingly turned yourselves into front-line beta microwave mug cake testers, packers, designers, proofreaders, and more … but what I mainly appreciate is your reaction to the idea of creating a gluten-free, healthier version of *101 Recipes for Microwave Mug Cakes*. You immediately opened your hearts and minds to the journey and shared it with me. How can I ever thank you enough?

INTRODUCTION

About two years ago, Barbara, a friend (and fellow cat lover) who lives nearly 3,000 miles away, emailed us a recipe she'd found online, by an anonymous source, for a single-serving chocolate mug cake that one could make in the microwave in less than five minutes. We tucked the recipe away for another time. Months later, an old college buddy, Pat, posted a link to the same recipe on his Facebook page.

We tried the chocolate mug cake. We liked it.

We created 101 original recipes to satisfy our craving for more simple snacks that would satisfy our need for a quick snack and wouldn't inflict a week's worth of leftovers on us. Thus, *101 Recipes for Microwave Mug Cakes: Single-Serving Snacks in Less Than 10 Minutes* was published, and the adventure began.

And now the adventure continues.

Our readers' enthusiastic reactions to our microwave mug cakes motivated us to reach beyond the original concept. We sensed a theme. Readers kept saying, "These recipes are wonderful, but are there more healthful alternatives? And is it possible to bake gluten-free microwave mug cakes?"

Our response to our readers' suggestions is *101 Recipes for Gluten-Free Microwave Mug Cakes: Healthier Single-Serving Snacks in Less Than 10 Minutes.*

Within these pages, you'll find a wealth of delicacies that nearly everyone (exempting true kitchenphobes) can easily and quickly prepare. You'll find a mix of recipes, that, in addition to being gluten-free, include snacks that may have one or more of the following properties: no added eggs, no added dairy products, no added sugar, or no added oil.

Check the icons at the top of each recipe to learn at a glance which are for you. (The index also organizes the recipes by ingredient category.)

OK, back to the kitchen. It will take a bit of preparation since some of the ingredients necessary to bake gluten-free microwave mug cakes are a bit exotic. We look forward to the day when supermarkets stock enough gluten-free baking products to satisfy everyone who is interested in exploring the benefits of gluten-free baking. In the meantime, we've provided a directory of online resources for ordering the gluten-free products that you'll need to create these recipes (see Resources).

As you've probably learned, microwave ovens are tricky beasts. We recommend that you stick closely to our recipes as well as our instructions for preparation. Please read those instructions. Our microwave oven suffered so that yours won't have to.

When's a good time to bake a gluten-free microwave mug cake?

- When you want a healthier snack
- When you deserve a reward that won't cause an allergic reaction
- When you want to discover a new treat with new textures and flavors
- When someone you care about has special dietary needs
- When you haven't enjoyed a homemade cake for way too long
- When you want to cheer someone up
- When you want to say "well done"
- When you want to say "thank you"
- When you want to say "I'm sorry"
- When you want to say "we're in this together"

It truly doesn't take any special skills or talents to bake a remarkably delicious gluten-free microwave mug cake. It does, however, take a bit of preparation to stock your pantry with gluten-free microwave mug cake-baking basics (some of them are easiest to locate online – more about that in the Resources section):

- gluten-free flours (including all-purpose, sorghum, millet, brown or white rice, almond, corn, coconut, fava bean, soy, amaranth, buckwheat, and quinoa)
- potato starch
- guar gum, xantham gum, or tapioca flour (these three ingredients can be used interchangeably in all of our gluten-free microwave mug cake recipes)
- flaxseed meal
- Domino® light brown sugar
- Argo® baking powder
- McCormick® extracts and ground spices
- soy milk, rice milk, almond milk, and milk (we prefer 1%)
- eggs
- apple cider vinegar
- Yoplait® Original yogurt
- JELL-O® pudding powder and gelatin powder
- cooking oil (we prefer canola)
- Minute® rice
- Skippy® peanut butter
- HERSHEY'S® semi-sweet chocolate chips and cocoa powder
- orange juice, apple juice, and lemon juice
- almond slivers, shredded coconut, and Sun-Maid® Natural Sun-Dried Raisins

- Grandma's® Original Molasses
- sorghum syrup (pure sorghum) and tapioca syrup
- Duncan Hines® frostings (all except Creamy Home-Style Coconut Pecan Frosting, which may contain gluten)
- Beech-Nut® baby foods
- Mott's® applesauce

The more ingredients you stock, the richer your potential variety of gluten-free MMCs will be. While you don't want to rush online and buy all the ingredients you'd need to make all 101 MMCs in this book at once, you do want to remember that shipping and handling costs can add up. Your local supermarket may have a good many of the products you'll need, too. And, if you adhere to a gluten-free diet (or someone in your home does), you may already have on hand a good many of the ingredients you'll need to make gluten-free microwave mug cakes.

Although we recommend particular brand products, you might prefer and trust other brands. If so, feel free to use them instead. At press time, the brands (and the specific products within those brands) are – according to their manufacturers – gluten-free. That can change, though, so always check with the company before you invest in their products.

It may be a while since you've indulged in a homemade sweet snack. If so, prepare to be amazed by what you can create in your favorite mug … in your own microwave oven … in less than ten minutes. Once you've read the GLUTEN-FREE MMC FAQs and GETTING STARTED, and once you've stocked up on the gluten-free ingredients you need to create these recipes, you'll be just ten minutes away from a sumptuous single-serving MMC snack.

Gluten-Free MMC FAQs

Q. What does "MMC" mean?

A. It stands for Microwave Mug Cake. Repeatedly typing, and saying, "Microwave Mug Cake" became too taxing for us after awhile, so we came up with MMC. Of course, this book focuses on gluten-free microwave mug cakes. But, to save space, we've usually abbreviated gluten-free microwave mug cake as "MMC."

Q. What's the difference between an MMC and a muffin?

A. An MMC looks a lot like a muffin, and when it's fresh from the microwave oven, it tastes just as good as a warm muffin. But an MMC takes far less time, energy, and equipment to prepare than a muffin does.

Q. What type of mug should I use?

A. You need a mug that can hold 16 ounces of liquid and, to create a solid MMC that can stand on its own, we suggest that you use a mug that's shaped like a cylinder. However, you may use a tapered mug if you don't mind a bit of wobbling.

Q. Do I have to remove my MMC from the mug before I eat it?

A. This has been a source of heated debate among intrepid MMC testers. There are two schools of thought. The first holds that fewer dishes are better, and as long as you wait about 5 minutes for a baked MMC to cool off, you can eat it directly from the mug. The second holds that you simply can't fit enough frosting on an MMC that's trapped in a mug, and unmolding the MMC before you eat it is a must. The choice is yours. Be warned, though, that since this is such a volatile subject, it's best not to bring the topic up anyplace where the volume of the conversation can be an issue.

Q. What do I do if my microwave mug cake breaks in half while I'm removing it from the mug?

A. Use frosting to "glue" it back together again, and relax. No one will care.

Q. Do I have to use the frosting and decoration combinations that you suggest in the "fancy stuff" portion of the recipes?

A. No. The suggestions are just that. Create your own favorite frostings and decorations, or eat the microwave mug cake bare. Have it the way you like it — it's your MMC!

Q. Do I have to measure the ingredients?

A. Please do. Because it only takes a small amount of ingredients to make an MMC, the proportions matter more than in other types of baking. "Eyeballing" the orange juice and pouring in a couple of "glops" may be fine if you're making a muffin. But the same glopping instead of precise measuring can cause the batter to spill over the mug and run all over your microwave. We're not trying to make your life difficult here. We're just trying to save your microwave oven — and your mug.

Q. Do I have to use a mixer and have a perfectly smooth batter?
A. No mixer is required, but do thoroughly mix the batter with a spoon or a whisk, and remove as many of the lumps as you can.

Q. Is it okay to use an egg substitute instead of an egg?
A. We'd say "no." Our intrepid MMC testers couldn't get egg substitutes to work, and they made many messes trying.

Q. What happens if I substitute, say, regular all-purpose flour for gluten-free all-purpose flour, or buckwheat flour for millet flour?
A. You do not want to substitute one flour for another unless you really, *really*, really know what you're doing. Each type of flour has its own density, flavor, and other properties. They are not interchangeable. Two tablespoons of sorghum flour do not necessarily equal two tablespoons of quinoa flour, nor does coconut flour have the same density as, say, millet flour. The only flours we consider interchangeable are brown and white rice flour. Take your pick, although we've found that brown rice flour lends a wonderfully rich, golden color to the finished MMC.

Q. All of the microwave mug cakes recipes say "1/2 teaspoon guar gum, xantham gum, or tapioca flour." Why is that?
A. All gluten-free microwave mug cake recipes require a thickener to replace the gluten. Guar gum, xantham gum, and tapioca flour all work equally well in the recipes. Choose whichever you prefer (or whichever is least expensive or most readily available).

Q. Some of the ingredients in the recipes specify "gluten-free," and some do not. Why is that?
A. We've specified "gluten-free" when failing to do so might have caused confusion. Anytime you're making gluten-free microwave mug cakes, all the ingredients you use should, of course, be gluten-free products.

Q. Are you sure that the products you've specified in these recipes are gluten-free?
A. No. We checked with the manufacturer of each product we mention and, in each case, were told that *as of that phone call or email exchange* the product was gluten-free. In numerous other cases, manufacturers of brands we know and routinely use assured us that their products were gluten-free – but that, for legal reasons, they weren't ready to make an official claim to that effect. Given that, and the fact that this is *your health and your family members' and friends' health* we're discussing, always check with the manufacturer for the most current gluten-related information for a product before you use it to make a gluten-free microwave mug cake.

Q. How can I store an uneaten portion of my microwave mug cake for another day?

A. Don't. By the next day, you can use the leftover MMC as a paperweight. Besides, you're always less than 10 minutes away from a new one. If you want to save some of your MMC for later the same day, however, you can try plastic wrap (or plastic ware) and hope for the best.

Q. Why do you suggest that I thump the batter-filled mug six times before baking it?

A. Because we felt that, on the seventh thump, you might break the mug. Seriously, thumping the mug firmly several times removes excess air bubbles and ensures that your finished gluten-free microwave mug cake won't end up lopsided.

Q. Should I add salt to the batter?

A. No. Microwave mug cakes don't require any salt.

Q. Vanilla extract: real or imitation?

A. We'd go with the real stuff. It's more expensive, but we think that it tastes better than the artificial flavoring.

Q. What type of milk do your recipes require?

A. We use 1% milk when a recipe calls for just "milk." Otherwise, we use soy milk, rice milk, or almond milk, as the recipe indicates.

Q. What type of oil should I use?

A. We use canola oil, and that turns out just fine. It's okay to use your favorite gluten-free cooking oil, but we'd steer clear of olive oil because of its pungent flavor.

Q. Is it okay to substitute white sugar in recipes that require light brown sugar?

A. We wouldn't, especially if you plan to eat your gluten-free MMC without frosting it (or to serve it to someone else). Since the microwave oven doesn't brown baked goods, the light brown sugar gives your MMC a finished look.

Q. What if I run out of an ingredient?

A. You can always substitute one flavor for another flavor of the same food type (the exception is, of course, flour – flours are not interchangeable). For example, you can use vanilla or chocolate pudding powder in place of pistachio pudding powder; you can swap lemon or mixed berry yogurt for strawberry yogurt. In fact, making these substitutions is a great way to unleash your creativity. Try it, and let us know what you come up with!

Q. What happens if I want to get really creative — say, adding an extra

two tablespoons of yogurt to a recipe, squirting in some pickle juice, or mixing together three different flavors of baby food?

A. Good luck with that — and *really* get ready to thoroughly clean up your microwave oven or forfeit your mug after your experiments in the event that things go wrong. In our experience, they probably will.

Q. Is this real baking, or is it a gimmick?

A. You're using real ingredients just like any gluten-free baker would. You're just reducing the time and portion size.

Q. Is it selfish to bake a gluten-free microwave mug cake for yourself?

A. Yes, but "selfish" isn't always a bad thing. Your loved ones want to see you happy, and if a gluten-free microwave mug cake can make your day, then go for it.

Q. How hot does the mug get once the MMC is baked?

A. Extremely hot. Wait two minutes before you remove the cake from the mug. And wait about five more minutes before you wash out the mug. Clean mugs are good. Burns are not.

Q. Must I use a fork to eat my gluten-free MMC?

A. Not unless you sense the neighbors are watching. Finger foods can be fun.

Q. What can I use to frost my gluten-free MMC?

A. In the first place, you can eat every MMC "as is." But, if you want to get into the fancy stuff, you can top your MMC with frosting (any gluten-free topping is fine), yogurt, and so forth. We have recommended specific frostings and toppings … but let your imagination be your guide.

Q. I'm unfamiliar with gluten-free baking. Is there a steep learning curve?

A. As long as you follow the recipes exactly, you'll be able to make a perfect gluten-free MMC the first time you try and every time thereafter. Later, you might expand your repertoire to include other types of gluten-free baking. But, for now, you can rest assured that you no longer have to deprive yourself of a delicious homemade snack just because you're on a gluten-free diet. Bring on the ingredients that are new to you, roll up your sleeves, and explore!

Q. Are you aware that the word "healthier" rightly applies only to living organisms – thus, recipes cannot actually be "healthier," and you're overtly and unabashedly misusing the word "healthier" in the subtitle of this book?

A. Yes. Thank you.

Q. Stacey, you wrote the book alone. Why, then, do you refer to yourself in the first person, plural, throughout the text?

A. We don't know, but it worries us.

GETTING STARTED

It's so simple to make a gluten-free microwave mug cake that it's almost too easy. Many intrepid MMC testers were so excited to get started that they failed to follow our directions the first time around. One of them spent the better part of an evening cleaning out her mug (which, sadly, she hadn't greased). To ensure that your MMC-baking experiences are all good ones, please read these notes from top to bottom before you bake your first MMC.

1. Wash and dry your mug before you begin, and thoroughly grease the inside. We use cooking spray, but butter or margarine work, too.

2. Place your mug on a saucer or plate before you bake it in the microwave. That way, if the batter runs over the top of the mug, the saucer or plate will catch the spills. (Obviously, you must use a microwave-safe mug and saucer/plate.)

3. Mix the batter in a medium-sized bowl and not directly in the mug. You don't need a mixer, but you do need to thoroughly mix the ingredients. We suggest you mix the wet ingredients together first, and then add the dry ingredients.

4. Fill your mug no more than halfway with batter. While the MMC is cooking, the batter may well rise beyond the top of the mug. It will fall again before it can cause a mess in your microwave, so do not be concerned, and do not stop your microwave's cooking process prematurely.

5. Use a microwave oven with a turntable, and bake your MMC on high power for between 3 and 4 minutes. Test your MMC with a toothpick to be sure it's done.

6. Use a potholder to remove your mug from the microwave. We're crazy about the Ove Glove™, because it allows your fingers complete flexibility and really does protect your hand.

7. Let the MMC cool for 2 minutes before you remove it from the mug. Let the mug cool for at least 5 minutes longer before you wash it.

8. Feel free to use the saucer or plate you placed under the mug to eat your unmolded MMC — provided you remembered to wash the bottom of the mug before placing it on the saucer or plate (or you have a very clean counter or table).

9. Time your MMC baking carefully. It's fine to bake yourself an MMC while you're at work when there's no one else in the break room. But, if someone else walks in, realize that you might have to share — and be prepared to give

up that which is yours in order to save a friendship or even your job.

10. Cool your MMC completely before you frost it, just as you would with a cake or muffin. Otherwise, be prepared to deal with a goopy, melted mess on your plate.

The Recipes

Almond Ambrosia Microwave Mug Cake

INGREDIENTS

1 egg
1 tablespoon apple cider vinegar
2 tablespoons almond milk
2 tablespoons oil
1/8 teaspoon McCormick® almond extract
  (or McCormick® vanilla extract)
1/4 teaspoon Argo® baking powder
1/2 teaspoon guar gum, xantham gum, or tapioca flour
1/2 teaspoon McCormick® ground cinnamon
4 tablespoons Domino® light brown sugar
3 tablespoons gluten-free sorghum flour
3 tablespoons gluten-free almond flour
3 tablespoons gluten-free all-purpose flour
2 tablespoons potato starch
2 tablespoons almond slivers

NOTE
If you make two Almond Ambrosia Microwave Mug Cakes, you have two of the Almond Brothers – or something very close.

DIRECTIONS

Prepare your microwavable mug by coating the inside lightly with cooking spray.

Mix the ingredients in a small bowl. Beat egg first with a spoon and mix in other liquid ingredients. Then add dry ingredients and mix until you've removed all the lumps.

Pour the batter into the mug (do not fill more than halfway) and smooth the top with a spoon. Thump mug firmly on the tabletop six times to remove excess air bubbles. Place mug on top of a microwavable small plate or saucer.

Bake for 3 - 4 minutes. Check for doneness by inserting a toothpick in the middle of the microwave mug cake and removing the toothpick. If the toothpick is dry, the MMC is done.

Wait 2 minutes, then run a butter knife along the inside of the mug, and tip the cake onto a plate. Position the mug cake so that the slightly rounded surface is on top. Your microwave mug cake will now look like a slightly overgrown muffin.

FANCY STUFF

Frost the whole Almond Ambrosia Microwave Mug Cake with Duncan Hines® Creamy Home-Style Classic Vanilla Frosting, or split the MMC in half, and frost each half individually (in which case you'll end up with two separate MMCs — or you can reassemble the frosted halves to create a layered MMC). Decorate, if you wish, with almond slivers.

Appearcot Microwave Mug Cake

INGREDIENTS
1 egg
4 tablespoons Beech-Nut® Apricots
   with Pears & Apples baby food
2 tablespoons Yoplait® Pear yogurt
1/8 teaspoon McCormick® vanilla extract
1/4 teaspoon Argo® baking powder
1/2 teaspoon guar gum, xantham gum, or tapioca flour
1/2 teaspoon McCormick® ground cinnamon
4 tablespoons Domino® light brown sugar
4 tablespoons gluten-free millet flour
4 tablespoons gluten-free brown or white rice flour
1 tablespoon potato starch

NOTE

If you got an apple, an apricot, and a pear in a room together, what would they have to say to one another?

DIRECTIONS
Prepare your microwavable mug by coating the inside lightly with cooking spray.

Mix the ingredients in a small bowl. Beat egg first with a spoon and mix in other liquid ingredients. Then add dry ingredients and mix until you've removed all the lumps.

Pour the batter into the mug (do not fill more than halfway) and smooth the top with a spoon. Thump mug firmly on the tabletop six times to remove excess air bubbles. Place mug on top of a microwavable small plate or saucer.

Bake for 3 - 4 minutes. Check for doneness by inserting a toothpick in the middle of the microwave mug cake and removing the toothpick. If the toothpick is dry, the MMC is done.

Wait 2 minutes, then run a butter knife along the inside of the mug, and tip the cake onto a plate. Position the mug cake so that the slightly rounded surface is on top. Your microwave mug cake will now look like a slightly overgrown muffin.

FANCY STUFF
Frost the whole Appearcot Microwave Mug Cake with Yoplait® Pear yogurt, or split the MMC in half, and frost each half individually (in which case you'll end up with two separate MMCs — or you can reassemble the frosted halves to create a layered MMC). Decorate, if you wish, with sliced pears or apricots.

Apple Almond Microwave Mug Cake

INGREDIENTS

1 egg
1 tablespoon Yoplait® French Vanilla yogurt
1 tablespoon apple cider vinegar
2 tablespoons apple juice
2 tablespoons oil
1/8 teaspoon McCormick® almond
extract (or McCormick® vanilla extract)
1/4 teaspoon Argo® baking powder
1/2 teaspoon guar gum, xantham gum, or tapioca flour
1/2 teaspoon McCormick® ground cinnamon
4 tablespoons Domino® light brown sugar
3 tablespoons gluten-free brown or white rice flour
3 tablespoons gluten-free almond flour
3 tablespoons gluten-free all-purpose flour
2 tablespoons potato starch

NOTE

During apple harvest time, you can climb a lot of trees in the crisp autumn air and pick yourself a bushel of apples. Either that, or you can just make yourself an Apple Almond Microwave Mug Cake.

DIRECTIONS

Prepare your microwavable mug by coating the inside lightly with cooking spray.

Mix the ingredients in a small bowl. Beat egg first with a spoon and mix in other liquid ingredients. Then add dry ingredients and mix until you've removed all the lumps.

Pour the batter into the mug (do not fill more than halfway) and smooth the top with a spoon. Thump mug firmly on the tabletop six times to remove excess air bubbles. Place mug on top of a microwavable small plate or saucer.

Bake for 3 - 4 minutes. Check for doneness by inserting a toothpick in the middle of the microwave mug cake and removing the toothpick. If the toothpick is dry, the MMC is done.

Wait 2 minutes, then run a butter knife along the inside of the mug, and tip the cake onto a plate. Position the mug cake so that the slightly rounded surface is on top. Your microwave mug cake will now look like a slightly overgrown muffin.

FANCY STUFF

Frost the whole Apple Almond Microwave Mug Cake with Mott's® applesauce, or split the MMC in half, and frost each half individually (in which case you'll end up with two separate MMCs — or you can reassemble the frosted halves to create a layered MMC). Decorate, if you wish, with sliced apples.

Apple Coffee Microwave Mug Cake

INGREDIENTS
1 egg
4 tablespoons Mott's® applesauce
3 tablespoons Yoplait® Coffee yogurt
1/8 teaspoon McCormick® almond
 extract (or McCormick® vanilla extract)
1/4 teaspoon Argo® baking powder
1/2 teaspoon guar gum, xantham gum, or tapioca flour
1/2 teaspoon instant coffee powder
4 tablespoons Domino® light brown sugar
2 tablespoons gluten-free coconut flour
2 tablespoons gluten-free almond flour
3 tablespoons gluten-free millet flour
1 tablespoon potato starch

NOTE
Wouldn't it be great if you could drink a cup of hot apple in the morning and bite into a crispy coffee?

DIRECTIONS
Prepare your microwavable mug by coating the inside lightly with cooking spray.

Mix the ingredients in a small bowl. Beat egg first with a spoon and mix in other liquid ingredients. Then add dry ingredients and mix until you've removed all the lumps.

Pour the batter into the mug (do not fill more than halfway) and smooth the top with a spoon. Thump mug firmly on the tabletop six times to remove excess air bubbles. Place mug on top of a microwavable small plate or saucer.

Bake for 3 - 4 minutes. Check for doneness by inserting a toothpick in the middle of the microwave mug cake and removing the toothpick. If the toothpick is dry, the MMC is done.

Wait 2 minutes, then run a butter knife along the inside of the mug, and tip the cake onto a plate. Position the mug cake so that the slightly rounded surface is on top. Your microwave mug cake will now look like a slightly overgrown muffin.

FANCY STUFF
Frost the whole Apple Coffee Microwave Mug Cake with Yoplait® Coffee yogurt, or split the MMC in half, and frost each half individually (in which case you'll end up with two separate MMCs — or you can reassemble the frosted halves to create a layered MMC). Decorate, if you wish, with sliced apples.

Appleach Microwave Mug Cake

INGREDIENTS

1 egg
2 tablespoons Beech-Nut® Peaches
baby food
2 tablespoons apple juice
2 tablespoons oil
2 tablespoons sorghum syrup (pure sorghum)
1/8 teaspoon McCormick® vanilla extract
1/4 teaspoon Argo® baking powder
1/2 teaspoon guar gum, xantham gum, or tapioca flour
1/2 teaspoon McCormick® ground cinnamon
4 tablespoons gluten-free sorghum flour
4 tablespoons gluten-free all-purpose flour
2 tablespoons potato starch

NOTE
An appleach a day would probably keep the doctor away – if there were any such thing as an appleach.

DIRECTIONS

Prepare your microwavable mug by coating the inside lightly with PAM Original cooking spray.

Mix the ingredients in a small bowl. Beat egg first with a spoon and mix in other liquid ingredients. Then add dry ingredients and mix until you've removed all the lumps.

Pour the batter into the mug (do not fill more than halfway) and smooth the top with a spoon. Thump mug firmly on the tabletop six times to remove excess air bubbles. Place mug on top of a microwavable small plate or saucer.

Bake for 3 - 4 minutes. Check for doneness by inserting a toothpick in the middle of the microwave mug cake and removing the toothpick. If the toothpick is dry, the MMC is done.

Wait 2 minutes, then run a butter knife along the inside of the mug, and tip the cake onto a plate. Position the mug cake so that the slightly rounded surface is on top. Your microwave mug cake will now look like a slightly overgrown muffin.

FANCY STUFF

Frost the whole Appleach Microwave Mug Cake with sorghum syrup, or split the MMC in half, and frost each half individually (in which case you'll end up with two separate MMCs — or you can reassemble the frosted halves to create a layered MMC). Decorate, if you wish, with sliced fruit.

Applenana Microwave Mug Cake

INGREDIENTS

1 egg
2 tablespoons Beech-Nut® Apples &
  Bananas baby food
4 tablespoons apple juice
2 tablespoons oil
1/8 teaspoon McCormick® vanilla extract
1/4 teaspoon Argo® baking powder
1/2 teaspoon guar gum, xantham gum, or tapioca flour
1/2 teaspoon McCormick® ground cinnamon
4 tablespoons Domino® light brown sugar
4 tablespoons gluten-free buckwheat flour
4 tablespoons gluten-free brown or white rice flour
1 tablespoon potato starch
2 tablespoons banana cream JELL-O® pudding powder

NOTE
Many apples, at some point, experience intense frustration when they realize they'll never be as slender as bananas. But then they grow out of it.

DIRECTIONS

Prepare your microwavable mug by coating the inside lightly with PAM Original cooking spray.

Mix the ingredients in a small bowl. Beat egg first with a spoon and mix in other liquid ingredients. Then add dry ingredients and mix until you've removed all the lumps.

Pour the batter into the mug (do not fill more than halfway) and smooth the top with a spoon. Thump mug firmly on the tabletop six times to remove excess air bubbles. Place mug on top of a microwavable small plate or saucer.

Bake for 3 - 4 minutes. Check for doneness by inserting a toothpick in the middle of the microwave mug cake and removing the toothpick. If the toothpick is dry, the MMC is done.

Wait 2 minutes, then run a butter knife along the inside of the mug, and tip the cake onto a plate. Position the mug cake so that the slightly rounded surface is on top. Your microwave mug cake will now look like a slightly overgrown muffin.

FANCY STUFF

Frost the whole Applenana Microwave Mug Cake with Duncan Hines® Creamy Home-Style Classic Vanilla Frosting, or split the MMC in half, and frost each half individually (in which case you'll end up with two separate MMCs — or you can reassemble the frosted halves to create a layered MMC). Decorate, if you wish, with sliced apples or bananas.

Applerry Microwave Mug Cake

INGREDIENTS

1 egg
2 tablespoons Beech-Nut® Apples &
   Cherries baby food
3 tablespoons milk
2 tablespoons oil
1/8 teaspoon McCormick® vanilla extract
1/4 teaspoon Argo® baking powder
1/2 teaspoon guar gum, xantham gum, or tapioca flour
1/2 teaspoon McCormick® ground cinnamon
4 tablespoons Domino® light brown sugar
3 tablespoons gluten-free brown or white rice flour
3 tablespoons gluten-free all-purpose flour
2 tablespoons potato starch

NOTE
How many times must you spin a
slot machine before you come up
with three applerrries?

DIRECTIONS

Prepare your microwavable mug by coating the inside lightly with PAM Original cooking spray.

Mix the ingredients in a small bowl. Beat egg first with a spoon and mix in other liquid ingredients. Then add dry ingredients and mix until you've removed all the lumps.

Pour the batter into the mug (do not fill more than halfway) and smooth the top with a spoon. Thump mug firmly on the tabletop six times to remove excess air bubbles. Place mug on top of a microwavable small plate or saucer.

Bake for 3 - 4 minutes. Check for doneness by inserting a toothpick in the middle of the microwave mug cake and removing the toothpick. If the toothpick is dry, the MMC is done.

Wait 2 minutes, then run a butter knife along the inside of the mug, and tip the cake onto a plate. Position the mug cake so that the slightly rounded surface is on top. Your microwave mug cake will now look like a slightly overgrown muffin.

FANCY STUFF

Frost the whole Applerry Microwave Mug Cake with Duncan Hines® Creamy Home-Style Butter Cream Frosting, or split the MMC in half, and frost each half individually (in which case you'll end up with two separate MMCs — or you can reassemble the frosted halves to create a layered MMC). Decorate, if you wish, with sliced fruit.

Banana Apple Microwave Mug Cake

INGREDIENTS

1 egg
2 tablespoons Mott's® applesauce
5 tablespoons apple juice
2 tablespoons oil
1/8 teaspoon McCormick® vanilla extract
1/4 teaspoon Argo® baking powder
1/2 teaspoon guar gum, xantham gum, or tapioca flour
1/2 teaspoon McCormick® ground cinnamon
4 tablespoons Domino® light brown sugar
4 tablespoons gluten-free amaranth flour
4 tablespoons gluten-free brown or white rice flour
1 tablespoon potato starch
2 tablespoons banana cream JELL-O® pudding powder

NOTE
Why don't comedians ever slip on apple peels?

DIRECTIONS

Prepare your microwavable mug by coating the inside lightly with PAM Original cooking spray.

Mix the ingredients in a small bowl. Beat egg first with a spoon and mix in other liquid ingredients. Then add dry ingredients and mix until you've removed all the lumps.

Pour the batter into the mug (do not fill more than halfway) and smooth the top with a spoon. Thump mug firmly on the tabletop six times to remove excess air bubbles. Place mug on top of a microwavable small plate or saucer.

Bake for 3 - 4 minutes. Check for doneness by inserting a toothpick in the middle of the microwave mug cake and removing the toothpick. If the toothpick is dry, the MMC is done.

Wait 2 minutes, then run a butter knife along the inside of the mug, and tip the cake onto a plate. Position the mug cake so that the slightly rounded surface is on top. Your microwave mug cake will now look like a slightly overgrown muffin.

FANCY STUFF

Frost the whole Banana Apple Microwave Mug Cake with Duncan Hines® Creamy Home-Style Butter Cream Frosting, or split the MMC in half, and frost each half individually (in which case you'll end up with two separate MMCs — or you can reassemble the frosted halves to create a layered MMC). Decorate, if you wish, with sliced apples or bananas.

Banana Bread Microwave Mug Cake

INGREDIENTS
1 egg
3 tablespoons Beech-Nut® Chiquita®
 Bananas baby food
3 tablespoons milk
2 tablespoons oil
1/8 teaspoon McCormick® banana
 extract (or McCormick® vanilla extract)
1/4 teaspoon Argo® baking powder
1/2 teaspoon guar gum, xantham gum, or tapioca flour
1/2 teaspoon McCormick® ground cinnamon
4 tablespoons Domino® light brown sugar
4 tablespoons gluten-free soy flour
4 tablespoons gluten-free sorghum flour
1 tablespoon potato starch
2 tablespoons banana cream JELL-O® pudding powder

NOTE
Five out of six monkeys surveyed prefer banana bread microwave mug cakes to actual bananas. One monkey explained, "When it comes out of the microwave, you don't even have to peel it."

DIRECTIONS
Prepare your microwavable mug by coating the inside lightly with PAM Original cooking spray.

Mix the ingredients in a small bowl. Beat egg first with a spoon and mix in other liquid ingredients. Then add dry ingredients and mix until you've removed all the lumps.

Pour the batter into the mug (do not fill more than halfway) and smooth the top with a spoon. Thump mug firmly on the tabletop six times to remove excess air bubbles. Place mug on top of a microwavable small plate or saucer.

Bake for 3 - 4 minutes. Check for doneness by inserting a toothpick in the middle of the microwave mug cake and removing the toothpick. If the toothpick is dry, the MMC is done.

Wait 2 minutes, then run a butter knife along the inside of the mug, and tip the cake onto a plate. Position the mug cake so that the slightly rounded surface is on top. Your microwave mug cake will now look like a slightly overgrown muffin.

FANCY STUFF
Frost the whole Banana Bread Microwave Mug Cake with Duncan Hines® Creamy Home-Style Butter Cream Frosting, or split the MMC in half, and frost each half individually (in which case you'll end up with two separate MMCs — or you can reassemble the frosted halves to create a layered MMC). Decorate, if you wish, with sliced bananas.

Banana Chocolate Chip Microwave Mug Cake

INGREDIENTS

1 egg

3 tablespoons rice milk

2 tablespoons oil

1/8 teaspoon McCormick® banana
   extract (or McCormick® vanilla extract)

1/4 teaspoon Argo® baking powder

1/2 teaspoon guar gum, xantham gum, or tapioca flour

4 tablespoons Domino® light brown sugar

5 tablespoons gluten-free brown or white rice flour

3 tablespoons gluten-free sorghum flour

1 tablespoon potato starch

2 tablespoons banana JELL-O® pudding powder

2 tablespoons HERSHEY'S® semi-sweet chocolate chips

NOTE

What happens if you cross rice with chocolate chips? You get rice with a chocolate chip on its shoulder! Either that, or you get a chip off the old block of rice.

DIRECTIONS

Prepare your microwavable mug by coating the inside lightly with PAM Original cooking spray.

Mix the ingredients in a small bowl. Beat egg first with a spoon and mix in other liquid ingredients. Then add dry ingredients and mix until you've removed all the lumps.

Pour the batter into the mug (do not fill more than halfway) and smooth the top with a spoon. Thump mug firmly on the tabletop six times to remove excess air bubbles. Place mug on top of a microwavable small plate or saucer.

Bake for 3 - 4 minutes. Check for doneness by inserting a toothpick in the middle of the microwave mug cake and removing the toothpick. If the toothpick is dry, the MMC is done.

Wait 2 minutes, then run a butter knife along the inside of the mug, and tip the cake onto a plate. Position the mug cake so that the slightly rounded surface is on top. Your microwave mug cake will now look like a slightly overgrown muffin.

FANCY STUFF

Frost the whole Banana Chocolate Chip Microwave Mug Cake with Duncan Hines® Creamy Home-Style Classic Chocolate Frosting, or split the MMC in half, and frost each half individually (in which case you'll end up with two separate MMCs — or you can reassemble the frosted halves to create a layered MMC). Decorate, if you wish, with HERSHEY'S® semi-sweet chocolate chips or sliced bananas.

Banana Coconut Microwave Mug Cake

INGREDIENTS

1 egg

2 tablespoons Beech-Nut® Chiquita®
Bananas baby food

4 tablespoons milk

2 tablespoons oil

1/8 teaspoon McCormick® coconut
extract (or McCormick® vanilla extract)

1/4 teaspoon Argo® baking powder

1/2 teaspoon guar gum, xantham gum, or tapioca flour

1/2 teaspoon McCormick® ground cinnamon

4 tablespoons Domino® light brown sugar

2 tablespoons gluten-free coconut flour

4 tablespoons gluten-free brown or white rice flour

2 tablespoons potato starch

2 tablespoons shredded coconut

DIRECTIONS

Prepare your microwavable mug by coating the inside lightly with PAM Original cooking spray.

Mix the ingredients in a small bowl. Beat egg first with a spoon and mix in other liquid ingredients. Then add dry ingredients and mix until you've removed all the lumps.

Pour the batter into the mug (do not fill more than halfway) and smooth the top with a spoon. Thump mug firmly on the tabletop six times to remove excess air bubbles. Place mug on top of a microwavable small plate or saucer.

Bake for 3 - 4 minutes. Check for doneness by inserting a toothpick in the middle of the microwave mug cake and removing the toothpick. If the toothpick is dry, the MMC is done.

Wait 2 minutes, then run a butter knife along the inside of the mug, and tip the cake onto a plate. Position the mug cake so that the slightly rounded surface is on top. Your microwave mug cake will now look like a slightly overgrown muffin.

FANCY STUFF

Frost the whole Banana Coconut Microwave Mug Cake with Duncan Hines® Creamy Home-Style Classic Vanilla Frosting, or split the MMC in half, and frost each half individually (in which case you'll end up with two separate MMCs — or you can reassemble the frosted halves to create a layered MMC). Decorate, if you wish, with shredded coconut.

Banana Ginger Microwave Mug Cake

INGREDIENTS
1 egg
2 tablespoons Beech-Nut® Chiquita®
  Bananas baby food
2 tablespoons oil
2 tablespoons Grandma's® Original Molasses
1/8 teaspoon McCormick® banana extract
  (or McCormick® vanilla extract)
1/4 teaspoon Argo® baking powder
1/2 teaspoon guar gum, xantham gum, or tapioca flour
1/2 teaspoon McCormick® ground ginger
1/4 teaspoon McCormick® ground cinnamon
pinch of McCormick® ground cloves
3 tablespoons Domino® light brown sugar
4 tablespoons gluten-free sorghum flour
4 tablespoons gluten-free all-purpose flour
1 tablespoon potato starch
2 tablespoons banana JELL-O® pudding powder

NOTE
If you were Gilligan, would you prefer Banana Ginger or Maryann Ginger? Just asking.

DIRECTIONS
Prepare your microwavable mug by coating the inside lightly with PAM Original cooking spray.

Mix the ingredients in a small bowl. Beat egg first with a spoon and mix in other liquid ingredients. Then add dry ingredients and mix until you've removed all the lumps.

Pour the batter into the mug (do not fill more than halfway) and smooth the top with a spoon. Thump mug firmly on the tabletop six times to remove excess air bubbles. Place mug on top of a microwavable small plate or saucer.

Bake for 3 - 4 minutes. Check for doneness by inserting a toothpick in the middle of the microwave mug cake and removing the toothpick. If the toothpick is dry, the MMC is done.

Wait 2 minutes, then run a butter knife along the inside of the mug, and tip the cake onto a plate. Position the mug cake so that the slightly rounded surface is on top. Your microwave mug cake will now look like a slightly overgrown muffin.

FANCY STUFF
Frost the whole Banana Ginger Microwave Mug Cake with Grandma's® Original Molasses, or split the MMC in half, and frost each half individually (in which case you'll end up with two separate MMCs — or you can reassemble the frosted halves to create a layered MMC). Top, if you wish, with whipped cream or sliced bananas.

Banana Soy Microwave Mug Cake

INGREDIENTS

1 egg
4 tablespoons Beech-Nut® Chiquita® Bananas baby food
3 tablespoons soy milk
1/8 teaspoon McCormick® vanilla extract
1/4 teaspoon Argo® baking powder
1/2 teaspoon guar gum, xantham gum, or tapioca flour
1/2 teaspoon McCormick® ground cinnamon
4 tablespoons Domino® light brown sugar
4 tablespoons gluten-free millet flour
4 tablespoons gluten-free brown or white rice flour
1 tablespoon potato starch

NOTE
Have you ever noticed that the word "soy" rhymes with "joy?" Can that be a mere coincidence?

DIRECTIONS

Prepare your microwavable mug by coating the inside lightly with cooking spray.

Mix the ingredients in a small bowl. Beat egg first with a spoon and mix in other liquid ingredients. Then add dry ingredients and mix until you've removed all the lumps.

Pour the batter into the mug (do not fill more than halfway) and smooth the top with a spoon. Thump mug firmly on the tabletop six times to remove excess air bubbles. Place mug on top of a microwavable small plate or saucer.

Bake for 3 - 4 minutes. Check for doneness by inserting a toothpick in the middle of the microwave mug cake and removing the toothpick. If the toothpick is dry, the MMC is done.

Wait 2 minutes, then run a butter knife along the inside of the mug, and tip the cake onto a plate. Position the mug cake so that the slightly rounded surface is on top. Your microwave mug cake will now look like a slightly overgrown muffin.

FANCY STUFF

Sprinkle Domino® light brown sugar on the whole Banana Soy Microwave Mug Cake, or split the MMC in half, and sprinkle each half individually (in which case you'll end up with two separate MMCs — or you can reassemble the sprinkled halves to create a layered MMC). Decorate, if you wish, with sliced bananas.

Blackberry Muffin Microwave Mug Cake

INGREDIENTS
1 egg
2 tablespoons Yoplait® Blackberry
  Harvest yogurt
2 tablespoons milk
2 tablespoons oil
1/8 teaspoon McCormick® vanilla extract
1/4 teaspoon Argo® baking powder
1/2 teaspoon guar gum, xantham gum, or tapioca flour
1/2 teaspoon McCormick® ground cinnamon
4 tablespoons Domino® light brown sugar
4 tablespoons gluten-free millet flour
4 tablespoons gluten-free sorghum flour
1 tablespoon potato starch
2 tablespoons vanilla JELL-O® pudding powder

NOTE
Well, that's the pot calling a kettle a blackberry. Or something like that.

DIRECTIONS
Prepare your microwavable mug by coating the inside lightly with PAM Original cooking spray.

Mix the ingredients in a small bowl. Beat egg first with a spoon and mix in other liquid ingredients. Then add dry ingredients and mix until you've removed all the lumps.

Pour the batter into the mug (do not fill more than halfway) and smooth the top with a spoon. Thump mug firmly on the tabletop six times to remove excess air bubbles. Place mug on top of a microwavable small plate or saucer.

Bake for 3 - 4 minutes. Check for doneness by inserting a toothpick in the middle of the microwave mug cake and removing the toothpick. If the toothpick is dry, the MMC is done.

Wait 2 minutes, then run a butter knife along the inside of the mug, and tip the cake onto a plate. Position the mug cake so that the slightly rounded surface is on top. Your microwave mug cake will now look like a slightly overgrown muffin.

FANCY STUFF
Frost the whole Blackberry Muffin Microwave Mug Cake with Yoplait® Blackberry Harvest yogurt, or split the MMC in half, and frost each half individually (in which case you'll end up with two separate MMCs — or you can reassemble the frosted halves to create a layered MMC). Decorate, if you wish, with sliced or whole berries.

Blueberry Coconut Microwave Mug Cake

INGREDIENTS
1 egg
2 tablespoons Yoplait® Mountain
Blueberry yogurt
3 tablespoons rice milk
2 tablespoons oil
1/8 teaspoon McCormick® coconut
extract (or McCormick® vanilla extract)
1/4 teaspoon Argo® baking powder
1/2 teaspoon guar gum, xantham gum, or tapioca flour
1/2 teaspoon McCormick® ground cinnamon
4 tablespoons Domino® light brown sugar
2 tablespoons gluten-free coconut flour
4 tablespoons gluten-free brown or white rice flour
2 tablespoons potato starch
2 tablespoons shredded coconut

NOTE

Out in nature, you can either pick blueberries, or you can pick coconuts. You can't pick both at the same time. You have to be in the supermarket to do that which is why supermarkets completely beat nature.

DIRECTIONS
Prepare your microwavable mug by coating the inside lightly with PAM Original cooking spray.

Mix the ingredients in a small bowl. Beat egg first with a spoon and mix in other liquid ingredients. Then add dry ingredients and mix until you've removed all the lumps.

Pour the batter into the mug (do not fill more than halfway) and smooth the top with a spoon. Thump mug firmly on the tabletop six times to remove excess air bubbles. Place mug on top of a microwavable small plate or saucer.

Bake for 3 - 4 minutes. Check for doneness by inserting a toothpick in the middle of the microwave mug cake and removing the toothpick. If the toothpick is dry, the MMC is done.

Wait 2 minutes, then run a butter knife along the inside of the mug, and tip the cake onto a plate. Position the mug cake so that the slightly rounded surface is on top. Your microwave mug cake will now look like a slightly overgrown muffin.

FANCY STUFF
Frost the whole Blueberry Coconut Microwave Mug Cake with Duncan Hines® Creamy Home-Style Classic Vanilla Frosting or Yoplait® Mountain Blueberry yogurt, or split the MMC in half, and frost each half individually (in which case you'll end up with two separate MMCs — or you can reassemble the frosted halves to create a layered MMC). Decorate, if you wish, with shredded coconut.

Blueberry Sorghum Microwave Mug Cake

INGREDIENTS
1 egg
2 tablespoons Yoplait® Mountain
  Blueberry yogurt
3 tablespoons milk
2 tablespoons oil
1/8 teaspoon McCormick® vanilla extract
1/4 teaspoon Argo® baking powder
1/2 teaspoon guar gum, xantham gum, or tapioca flour
1 tablespoon sorghum syrup (pure sorghum)
1/2 teaspoon McCormick® ground cinnamon
1 tablespoon gluten-free coconut flour
3 tablespoons gluten-free brown or white rice flour
4 tablespoons gluten-free sorghum flour
1 tablespoon potato starch
2 tablespoons vanilla JELL-O® pudding powder

NOTE
Five out of six blueberries surveyed said they'd rather be syruped than arrested.

DIRECTIONS
Prepare your microwavable mug by coating the inside lightly with PAM Original cooking spray.

Mix the ingredients in a small bowl. Beat egg first with a spoon and mix in other liquid ingredients. Then add dry ingredients and mix until you've removed all the lumps.

Pour the batter into the mug (do not fill more than halfway) and smooth the top with a spoon. Thump mug firmly on the tabletop six times to remove excess air bubbles. Place mug on top of a microwavable small plate or saucer.

Bake for 3 - 4 minutes. Check for doneness by inserting a toothpick in the middle of the microwave mug cake and removing the toothpick. If the toothpick is dry, the MMC is done.

Wait 2 minutes, then run a butter knife along the inside of the mug, and tip the cake onto a plate. Position the mug cake so that the slightly rounded surface is on top. Your microwave mug cake will now look like a slightly overgrown muffin.

FANCY STUFF
Frost the whole the Blueberry Sorghum Microwave Mug Cake with Yoplait® Mountain Blueberry yogurt or Duncan Hines® Creamy Home-Style Classic Vanilla Frosting, or split the MMC in half, and frost each half individually (in which case you'll end up with two separate MMCs — or you can reassemble the frosted halves to create a layered MMC). Decorate, if you wish, with shredded coconut.

Butterscotch Coconut Microwave Mug Cake

INGREDIENTS
1 egg
2 tablespoons Yoplait® French Vanilla yogurt
3 tablespoons rice milk
2 tablespoons oil
1/8 teaspoon McCormick® coconut extract (or McCormick® vanilla extract)
1/4 teaspoon Argo® baking powder
1/2 teaspoon guar gum, xantham gum, or tapioca flour
1/2 teaspoon McCormick® ground cinnamon
4 tablespoons Domino® light brown sugar
2 tablespoons gluten-free coconut flour
4 tablespoons gluten-free all-purpose flour
1 tablespoon potato starch
2 tablespoons butterscotch JELL-O® pudding powder
2 tablespoons shredded coconut

NOTE
Ever wish you could buy butterscotch-flavored coconuts in the produce aisle? Well, maybe someday….

DIRECTIONS
Prepare your microwavable mug by coating the inside lightly with PAM Original cooking spray.

Mix the ingredients in a small bowl. Beat egg first with a spoon and mix in other liquid ingredients. Then add dry ingredients and mix until you've removed all the lumps.

Pour the batter into the mug (do not fill more than halfway) and smooth the top with a spoon. Thump mug firmly on the tabletop six times to remove excess air bubbles. Place mug on top of a microwavable small plate or saucer.

Bake for 3 - 4 minutes. Check for doneness by inserting a toothpick in the middle of the microwave mug cake and removing the toothpick. If the toothpick is dry, the MMC is done.

Wait 2 minutes, then run a butter knife along the inside of the mug, and tip the cake onto a plate. Position the mug cake so that the slightly rounded surface is on top. Your microwave mug cake will now look like a slightly overgrown muffin.

FANCY STUFF
Frost the whole Butterscotch Coconut Microwave Mug Cake with Duncan Hines® Creamy Home-Style Caramel Frosting, or split the MMC in half, and frost each half individually (in which case you'll end up with two separate MMCs — or you can reassemble the frosted halves to create a layered MMC). Decorate, if you wish, with shredded coconut.

Butterscotch Coffee Microwave Mug Cake

INGREDIENTS

1 egg
4 tablespoons Mott's® applesauce
3 tablespoons Yoplait® Coffee yogurt
1/8 teaspoon McCormick® vanilla extract
1/4 teaspoon Argo® baking powder
1/2 teaspoon guar gum, xantham gum,
  or tapioca flour
1/2 teaspoon instant coffee powder
4 tablespoons Domino® light brown sugar
4 tablespoons gluten-free sorghum flour
4 tablespoons gluten-free soy flour
1 tablespoon potato starch
2 tablespoons butterscotch JELL-O® pudding powder

NOTE
Have you ever tried drinking butterscotch while munching on coffee? It isn't as easy as it looks, is it?

DIRECTIONS

Prepare your microwavable mug by coating the inside lightly with cooking spray.

Mix the ingredients in a small bowl. Beat egg first with a spoon and mix in other liquid ingredients. Then add dry ingredients and mix until you've removed all the lumps.

Pour the batter into the mug (do not fill more than halfway) and smooth the top with a spoon. Thump mug firmly on the tabletop six times to remove excess air bubbles. Place mug on top of a microwavable small plate or saucer.

Bake for 3 - 4 minutes. Check for doneness by inserting a toothpick in the middle of the microwave mug cake and removing the toothpick. If the toothpick is dry, the MMC is done.

Wait 2 minutes, then run a butter knife along the inside of the mug, and tip the cake onto a plate. Position the mug cake so that the slightly rounded surface is on top. Your microwave mug cake will now look like a slightly overgrown muffin.

FANCY STUFF

Frost the whole Butterscotch Coffee Microwave Mug Cake with Yoplait® Coffee yogurt, or split the MMC in half, and frost each half individually (in which case you'll end up with two separate MMCs — or you can reassemble the frosted halves to create a layered MMC). Decorate, if you wish, with sliced apples.

Butterscotch Ginger Microwave Mug Cake

INGREDIENTS

1 egg
3 tablespoons rice milk
2 tablespoons oil
1/8 teaspoon McCormick® vanilla extract
1/4 teaspoon Argo® baking powder
1/2 teaspoon guar gum, xantham gum, or tapioca flour
1/2 teaspoon ginger
4 tablespoons Domino® light brown sugar
5 tablespoons gluten-free brown or white rice flour
3 tablespoons gluten-free sorghum flour
1 tablespoon potato starch
2 tablespoons butterscotch JELL-O® pudding powder

NOTE
Where does butterscotch come from? Scotland, obviously! Or maybe Butterland.

DIRECTIONS

Prepare your microwavable mug by coating the inside lightly with PAM Original cooking spray.

Mix the ingredients in a small bowl. Beat egg first with a spoon and mix in other liquid ingredients. Then add dry ingredients and mix until you've removed all the lumps.

Pour the batter into the mug (do not fill more than halfway) and smooth the top with a spoon. Thump mug firmly on the tabletop six times to remove excess air bubbles. Place mug on top of a microwavable small plate or saucer.

Bake for 3 - 4 minutes. Check for doneness by inserting a toothpick in the middle of the microwave mug cake and removing the toothpick. If the toothpick is dry, the MMC is done.

Wait 2 minutes, then run a butter knife along the inside of the mug, and tip the cake onto a plate. Position the mug cake so that the slightly rounded surface is on top. Your microwave mug cake will now look like a slightly overgrown muffin.

FANCY STUFF

Frost the whole Butterscotch Ginger Microwave Mug Cake with Duncan Hines® Creamy Home-Style Caramel Frosting, or split the MMC in half, and frost each half individually (in which case you'll end up with two separate MMCs — or you can reassemble the frosted halves to create a layered MMC). Decorate, if you wish, with Sun-Maid® Natural Sun-Dried Raisins.

Cherregranate Chip Microwave Mug Cake

INGREDIENTS
1 egg
3 tablespoons Yoplait®
  Cherry Pomegranate yogurt
3 tablespoons milk
2 tablespoons oil
1/8 teaspoon McCormick® vanilla extract
1/4 teaspoon Argo® baking powder
1/2 teaspoon guar gum, xantham gum, or tapioca flour
1/2 teaspoon McCormick® ground cinnamon
4 tablespoons Domino® light brown sugar
4 tablespoons gluten-free soy flour
4 tablespoons gluten-free sorghum flour
2 tablespoons potato starch
2 tablespoons HERSHEY'S® semi-sweet chocolate chips

NOTE
Doesn't it strike you as slightly unfair that cherries have one pit apiece while pomegranates have dozens, if not hundreds, of them?

DIRECTIONS
Prepare your microwavable mug by coating the inside lightly with PAM Original cooking spray.

Mix the ingredients in a small bowl. Beat egg first with a spoon and mix in other liquid ingredients. Then add dry ingredients and mix until you've removed all the lumps.

Pour the batter into the mug (do not fill more than halfway) and smooth the top with a spoon. Thump mug firmly on the tabletop six times to remove excess air bubbles. Place mug on top of a microwavable small plate or saucer.

Bake for 3 - 4 minutes. Check for doneness by inserting a toothpick in the middle of the microwave mug cake and removing the toothpick. If the toothpick is dry, the MMC is done.

Wait 2 minutes, then run a butter knife along the inside of the mug, and tip the cake onto a plate. Position the mug cake so that the slightly rounded surface is on top. Your microwave mug cake will now look like a slightly overgrown muffin.

FANCY STUFF
Frost the whole Cherregranate Chip Microwave Mug Cake with Yoplait® Cherry Pomegranate yogurt or Duncan Hines® Creamy Home-Style Classic Vanilla Frosting, or split the MMC in half, and frost each half individually (in which case you'll end up with two separate MMCs — or you can reassemble the frosted halves to create a layered MMC). Decorate, if you wish, with HERSHEY'S® semi-sweet chocolate chips.

Choco Pear Microwave Mug Cake

INGREDIENTS

1 egg
2 tablespoons Beech-Nut® Pears baby food
5 tablespoons milk
2 tablespoons oil
1/8 teaspoon McCormick® vanilla extract
1/4 teaspoon Argo® baking powder
1/2 teaspoon guar gum, xantham gum, or tapioca flour
1/2 teaspoon McCormick® ground cinnamon
4 tablespoons Domino® light brown sugar
1 tablespoon gluten-free coconut flour
3 tablespoons gluten-free brown or white rice flour
4 tablespoons gluten-free sorghum flour
1 tablespoon potato starch
2 tablespoons white chocolate JELL-O® pudding powder

NOTE
Objects in microwave ovens may be closer than they a pear. Get it? A pear? Never mind.

DIRECTIONS

Prepare your microwavable mug by coating the inside lightly with PAM Original cooking spray.

Mix the ingredients in a small bowl. Beat egg first with a spoon and mix in other liquid ingredients. Then add dry ingredients and mix until you've removed all the lumps.

Pour the batter into the mug (do not fill more than halfway) and smooth the top with a spoon. Thump mug firmly on the tabletop six times to remove excess air bubbles. Place mug on top of a microwavable small plate or saucer.

Bake for 3 - 4 minutes. Check for doneness by inserting a toothpick in the middle of the microwave mug cake and removing the toothpick. If the toothpick is dry, the MMC is done.

Wait 2 minutes, then run a butter knife along the inside of the mug, and tip the cake onto a plate. Position the mug cake so that the slightly rounded surface is on top. Your microwave mug cake will now look like a slightly overgrown muffin.

FANCY STUFF

Frost the whole the Choco Pear Microwave Mug Cake with Duncan Hines® Creamy Home-Style Classic Chocolate Frosting, or split the MMC in half, and frost each half individually (in which case you'll end up with two separate MMCs — or you can reassemble the frosted halves to create a layered MMC). Decorate, if you wish, with sliced pears.

Chocolate Almond Microwave Mug Cake

INGREDIENTS
1 egg
1 tablespoon apple cider vinegar
2 tablespoons Mott's® applesauce
1 tablespoon almond milk
2 tablespoons oil
1/8 teaspoon McCormick® almond extract
   (or McCormick® vanilla extract)
1/4 teaspoon Argo® baking powder
1/2 teaspoon guar gum, xantham gum, or tapioca flour
1/2 teaspoon McCormick® ground cinnamon
4 tablespoons Domino® light brown sugar
5 tablespoons gluten-free almond flour
3 tablespoons gluten-free sorghum flour
2 tablespoons HERSHEY'S® cocoa powder
2 tablespoons almond slivers

NOTE
Why does chocolate always get top billing when you combine chocolate and almonds? It just doesn't seem fair, somehow.

DIRECTIONS
Prepare your microwavable mug by coating the inside lightly with PAM Original cooking spray.

Mix the ingredients in a small bowl. Beat egg first with a spoon and mix in other liquid ingredients. Then add dry ingredients and mix until you've removed all the lumps.

Pour the batter into the mug (do not fill more than halfway) and smooth the top with a spoon. Thump mug firmly on the tabletop six times to remove excess air bubbles. Place mug on top of a microwavable small plate or saucer.

Bake for 3 - 4 minutes. Check for doneness by inserting a toothpick in the middle of the microwave mug cake and removing the toothpick. If the toothpick is dry, the MMC is done.

Wait 2 minutes, then run a butter knife along the inside of the mug, and tip the cake onto a plate. Position the mug cake so that the slightly rounded surface is on top. Your microwave mug cake will now look like a slightly overgrown muffin.

FANCY STUFF
Frost the whole Chocolate Almond Microwave Mug Cake with Duncan Hines® Creamy Home-Style Classic Chocolate Frosting, or split the MMC in half, and frost each half individually (in which case you'll end up with two separate MMCs — or you can reassemble the frosted halves to create a layered MMC). Decorate, if you wish, with HERSHEY'S® semi-sweet chocolate chips.

Chocolate Apple Cherry Microwave Mug Cake

INGREDIENTS

1 egg
2 tablespoons Beech-Nut® Apples &
  Cherries baby food
2 tablespoon milk
2 tablespoons oil
1/8 teaspoon McCormick® vanilla extract
1/4 teaspoon Argo® baking powder
1/2 teaspoon guar gum, xantham gum, or tapioca flour
1/2 teaspoon McCormick® ground cinnamon
4 tablespoons Domino® light brown sugar
4 tablespoons gluten-free sorghum flour
4 tablespoons gluten-free millet flour
1 tablespoon potato starch
2 tablespoons HERSHEY'S® cocoa powder

NOTE

Why is it that apples and cherries only come into season simultaneously in a jar or in a mug?

DIRECTIONS

Prepare your microwavable mug by coating the inside lightly with PAM Original cooking spray.

Mix the ingredients in a small bowl. Beat egg first with a spoon and mix in other liquid ingredients. Then add dry ingredients and mix until you've removed all the lumps.

Pour the batter into the mug (do not fill more than halfway) and smooth the top with a spoon. Thump mug firmly on the tabletop six times to remove excess air bubbles. Place mug on top of a microwavable small plate or saucer.

Bake for 3 - 4 minutes. Check for doneness by inserting a toothpick in the middle of the microwave mug cake and removing the toothpick. If the toothpick is dry, the MMC is done.

Wait 2 minutes, then run a butter knife along the inside of the mug, and tip the cake onto a plate. Position the mug cake so that the slightly rounded surface is on top. Your microwave mug cake will now look like a slightly overgrown muffin.

FANCY STUFF

Frost the whole Chocolate Apple Cherry Microwave Mug Cake with Duncan Hines® Creamy Home-Style Classic Chocolate Frosting, or split the MMC in half, and frost each half individually (in which case you'll end up with two separate MMCs — or you can reassemble the frosted halves to create a layered MMC). Decorate, if you wish, with sliced apples or sliced cherries.

Chocolate Chip Carrot Microwave Mug Cake

NO ADDED DAIRY

INGREDIENTS

1 egg

2 tablespoons Beech-Nut® Tender Sweet Carrots baby food

4 tablespoons soy milk

2 tablespoons oil

1/8 teaspoon McCormick® vanilla extract

1/4 teaspoon Argo® baking powder

1/2 teaspoon guar gum, xantham gum, or tapioca flour

1/2 teaspoon McCormick® ground cinnamon

4 tablespoons Domino® light brown sugar

2 tablespoons gluten-free amaranth flour

6 tablespoons gluten-free millet flour

2 tablespoons potato starch

2 tablespoons HERSHEY'S® semi-sweet chocolate chips

NOTE
Why doesn't anyone ever bake with carrot chips?

DIRECTIONS

Prepare your microwavable mug by coating the inside lightly with PAM Original cooking spray.

Mix the ingredients in a small bowl. Beat egg first with a spoon and mix in other liquid ingredients. Then add dry ingredients and mix until you've removed all the lumps.

Pour the batter into the mug (do not fill more than halfway) and smooth the top with a spoon. Thump mug firmly on the tabletop six times to remove excess air bubbles. Place mug on top of a microwavable small plate or saucer.

Bake for 3 - 4 minutes. Check for doneness by inserting a toothpick in the middle of the microwave mug cake and removing the toothpick. If the toothpick is dry, the MMC is done.

Wait 2 minutes, then run a butter knife along the inside of the mug, and tip the cake onto a plate. Position the mug cake so that the slightly rounded surface is on top. Your microwave mug cake will now look like a slightly overgrown muffin.

FANCY STUFF

Frost the whole Chocolate Chip Carrot Microwave Mug Cake with Duncan Hines® Creamy Home-Style Cream Cheese Frosting, or split the MMC in half, and frost each half individually (in which case you'll end up with two separate MMCs — or you can reassemble the frosted halves to create a layered MMC). Decorate, if you wish, with HERSHEY'S® semi-sweet chocolate chips.

Chocolate Chip Orange Microwave Mug Cake

INGREDIENTS
1 tablespoon apple cider vinegar
1 tablespoon flaxseed meal
2 tablespoons Yoplait® French Vanilla yogurt
5 tablespoons orange juice
2 tablespoons oil
1/8 teaspoon McCormick® vanilla extract
1/4 teaspoon Argo® baking powder
1/2 teaspoon guar gum, xantham gum, or tapioca flour
1/2 teaspoon McCormick® ground cinnamon
4 tablespoons Domino® light brown sugar
4 tablespoons gluten-free soy flour
4 tablespoons gluten-free sorghum flour
2 tablespoons potato starch
2 tablespoons HERSHEY'S® semi-sweet chocolate chips

NOTE
*Name something that rhymes
with chocolate chip orange.*

DIRECTIONS
Prepare your microwavable mug by coating the inside lightly with PAM
Original cooking spray.

Mix the ingredients in a small bowl. Add flaxseed meal to liquid ingredients
and beat together. Then add dry ingredients and mix until you've removed
all the lumps.

Pour the batter into the mug (do not fill more than halfway) and smooth the
top with a spoon. Thump mug firmly on the tabletop six times to remove
excess air bubbles. Place mug on top of a microwavable small plate or saucer.

Bake for 3 - 4 minutes. Check for doneness by inserting a toothpick in the
middle of the microwave mug cake and removing the toothpick. If the
toothpick is dry, the MMC is done.

Wait 2 minutes, then run a butter knife along the inside of the mug, and tip
the cake onto a plate. Position the mug cake so that the slightly rounded
surface is on top. Your microwave mug cake will now look like a slightly
overgrown muffin.

FANCY STUFF
Frost the whole Chocolate Chip Orange Microwave Mug Cake with Duncan
Hines® Creamy Home-Style Classic Chocolate Frosting, or split the MMC in
half, and frost each half individually (in which case you'll end up with two
separate MMCs — or you can reassemble the frosted halves to create a
layered MMC). Decorate, if you wish, with HERSHEY'S® semi-sweet chocolate
chips.

Chocolate Chip Sorghum Microwave Mug Cake

INGREDIENTS
1 egg
2 tablespoons Yoplait® French Vanilla yogurt
3 tablespoons soy milk
2 tablespoons oil
1/8 teaspoon McCormick® vanilla extract
1/4 teaspoon Argo® baking powder
1/2 teaspoon guar gum, xantham gum, or tapioca flour
1 tablespoon sorghum syrup (pure sorghum)
3 tablespoons gluten-free almond flour
5 tablespoons gluten-free brown or white rice flour
1 tablespoon potato starch
2 tablespoons HERSHEY'S® semi-sweet chocolate chips

NOTE
Did you ever wonder why they don't make sorghum syrup chips? Hmm…

DIRECTIONS
Prepare your microwavable mug by coating the inside lightly with PAM Original cooking spray.

Mix the ingredients in a small bowl. Beat egg first with a spoon and mix in other liquid ingredients. Then add dry ingredients and mix until you've removed all the lumps.

Pour the batter into the mug (do not fill more than halfway) and smooth the top with a spoon. Thump mug firmly on the tabletop six times to remove excess air bubbles. Place mug on top of a microwavable small plate or saucer.

Bake for 3 - 4 minutes. Check for doneness by inserting a toothpick in the middle of the microwave mug cake and removing the toothpick. If the toothpick is dry, the MMC is done.

Wait 2 minutes, then run a butter knife along the inside of the mug, and tip the cake onto a plate. Position the mug cake so that the slightly rounded surface is on top. Your microwave mug cake will now look like a slightly overgrown muffin.

FANCY STUFF
Frost the whole Chocolate Chip Sorghum Microwave Mug Cake with sorghum syrup (pure sorghum), or split the MMC in half, and frost each half individually (in which case you'll end up with two separate MMCs — or you can reassemble the frosted halves to create a layered MMC). Decorate, if you wish, with HERSHEY'S® semi-sweet chocolate chips.

Chocolate Mango Microwave Mug Cake

INGREDIENTS

1 egg

2 tablespoons Beech-Nut® Mango
  baby food

4 tablespoons milk

2 tablespoons oil

1/8 teaspoon McCormick® vanilla extract

1/4 teaspoon Argo® baking powder

1/2 teaspoon guar gum, xantham gum, or tapioca flour

1/2 teaspoon McCormick® ground cinnamon

4 tablespoons Domino® light brown sugar

4 tablespoons gluten-free fava bean flour

4 tablespoons gluten-free brown or white rice flour

2 tablespoons HERSHEY'S® cocoa powder

NOTE
Why are they called mangos
instead of humangos?

DIRECTIONS

Prepare your microwavable mug by coating the inside lightly with PAM Original cooking spray.

Mix the ingredients in a small bowl. Beat egg first with a spoon and mix in other liquid ingredients. Then add dry ingredients and mix until you've removed all the lumps.

Pour the batter into the mug (do not fill more than halfway) and smooth the top with a spoon. Thump mug firmly on the tabletop six times to remove excess air bubbles. Place mug on top of a microwavable small plate or saucer.

Bake for 3 - 4 minutes. Check for doneness by inserting a toothpick in the middle of the microwave mug cake and removing the toothpick. If the toothpick is dry, the MMC is done.

Wait 2 minutes, then run a butter knife along the inside of the mug, and tip the cake onto a plate. Position the mug cake so that the slightly rounded surface is on top. Your microwave mug cake will now look like a slightly overgrown muffin.

FANCY STUFF

Frost the whole Chocolate Mango Microwave Mug Cake with Duncan Hines® Creamy Home-Style Milk Chocolate Frosting, or split the MMC in half, and frost each half individually (in which case you'll end up with two separate MMCs — or you can reassemble the frosted halves to create a layered MMC). Decorate, if you wish, with sliced fruit.

Chocolate Pineapple Microwave Mug Cake

INGREDIENTS
1 egg
2 tablespoons Yoplait® Pineapple yogurt
1 tablespoon milk
2 tablespoons oil
1/8 teaspoon McCormick® vanilla extract
1/4 teaspoon Argo® baking powder
1/2 teaspoon guar gum, xantham gum, or tapioca flour
1/2 teaspoon McCormick® ground cinnamon
4 tablespoons Domino® light brown sugar
4 tablespoons gluten-free sorghum flour
4 tablespoons gluten-free millet flour
1 tablespoon potato starch
2 tablespoons HERSHEY'S® cocoa powder

NOTE
Do chocolate-covered pineapples feel any different from, say, their strawberry-covered pineapple sisters? That would be a great question to ask a pineapple.

DIRECTIONS
Prepare your microwavable mug by coating the inside lightly with PAM Original cooking spray.

Mix the ingredients in a small bowl. Beat egg first with a spoon and mix in other liquid ingredients. Then add dry ingredients and mix until you've removed all the lumps.

Pour the batter into the mug (do not fill more than halfway) and smooth the top with a spoon. Thump mug firmly on the tabletop six times to remove excess air bubbles. Place mug on top of a microwavable small plate or saucer.

Bake for 3 - 4 minutes. Check for doneness by inserting a toothpick in the middle of the microwave mug cake and removing the toothpick. If the toothpick is dry, the MMC is done.

Wait 2 minutes, then run a butter knife along the inside of the mug, and tip the cake onto a plate. Position the mug cake so that the slightly rounded surface is on top. Your microwave mug cake will now look like a slightly overgrown muffin.

FANCY STUFF
Frost the whole Chocolate Pineapple Microwave Mug Cake with Yoplait® Pineapple yogurt or Duncan Hines® Creamy Home-Style Classic Chocolate Frosting, or split the MMC in half, and frost each half individually (in which case you'll end up with two separate MMCs — or you can reassemble the frosted halves to create a layered MMC). Decorate, if you wish, with pineapple chunks.

Chocolate Pumpkin Microwave Mug Cake

INGREDIENTS

1 egg
2 tablespoons canned pumpkin
2 tablespoons Yoplait® French
  Vanilla yogurt
5 tablespoons milk
2 tablespoons oil
1/8 teaspoon McCormick® vanilla extract
1/4 teaspoon Argo® baking powder
1/2 teaspoon guar gum, xantham gum, or tapioca flour
1/2 teaspoon McCormick® ground cinnamon
4 tablespoons Domino® light brown sugar
4 tablespoons gluten-free sorghum flour
4 tablespoons gluten-free brown or white rice flour
1 tablespoon potato starch
2 tablespoons HERSHEY'S® cocoa powder

NOTE
Is it really Autumn if you don't figure out a way to get hold of a chocolate pumpkin?

DIRECTIONS

Prepare your microwavable mug by coating the inside lightly with PAM Original cooking spray.

Mix the ingredients in a small bowl. Beat egg first with a spoon and mix in other liquid ingredients. Then add dry ingredients and mix until you've removed all the lumps.

Pour the batter into the mug (do not fill more than halfway) and smooth the top with a spoon. Thump mug firmly on the tabletop six times to remove excess air bubbles. Place mug on top of a microwavable small plate or saucer.

Bake for 3 - 4 minutes. Check for doneness by inserting a toothpick in the middle of the microwave mug cake and removing the toothpick. If the toothpick is dry, the MMC is done.

Wait 2 minutes, then run a butter knife along the inside of the mug, and tip the cake onto a plate. Position the mug cake so that the slightly rounded surface is on top. Your microwave mug cake will now look like a slightly overgrown muffin.

FANCY STUFF

Frost the whole Chocolate Pumpkin Microwave Mug Cake with Duncan Hines® Creamy Home-Style Classic Chocolate Frosting, or split the MMC in half, and frost each half individually (in which case you'll end up with two separate MMCs — or you can reassemble the frosted halves to create a layered MMC). Decorate, if you wish, with your choice of sliced fruit or gluten-free candies.

Chocolateberry Microwave Mug Cake

INGREDIENTS

1 tablespoon apple cider vinegar
1 tablespoon flaxseed meal
2 tablespoons Beech-Nut® Apples & Blueberries baby food
5 tablespoons milk
2 tablespoons Yoplait® Blackberry Harvest yogurt
2 tablespoons oil
1/8 teaspoon McCormick® vanilla extract
1/4 teaspoon Argo® baking powder
1/2 teaspoon guar gum, xantham gum, or tapioca flour
1/2 teaspoon McCormick® ground cinnamon
4 tablespoons Domino® light brown sugar
1 tablespoon gluten-free coconut flour
3 tablespoons gluten-free brown or white rice flour
4 tablespoons gluten-free sorghum flour
2 tablespoons potato starch
2 tablespoons HERSHEY'S® semi-sweet chocolate chips

NOTE
Berries are somehow made for chocolate. It's therefore odd that berries aren't shaped like candy bars.

DIRECTIONS

Prepare your microwavable mug by coating the inside lightly with PAM Original cooking spray.

Mix the ingredients in a small bowl. Add flaxseed meal to liquid ingredients and beat together. Then add dry ingredients and mix until you've removed all the lumps.

Pour the batter into the mug (do not fill more than halfway) and smooth the top with a spoon. Thump mug firmly on the tabletop six times to remove excess air bubbles. Place mug on top of a microwavable small plate or saucer.

Bake for 3 - 4 minutes. Check for doneness by inserting a toothpick in the middle of the microwave mug cake and removing the toothpick. If the toothpick is dry, the MMC is done.

Wait 2 minutes, then run a butter knife along the inside of the mug, and tip the cake onto a plate. Position the mug cake so that the slightly rounded surface is on top. Your microwave mug cake will now look like a slightly overgrown muffin.

FANCY STUFF

Frost the whole Chocolateberry Microwave Mug Cake with Duncan Hines® Creamy Home-Style Classic Chocolate Frosting, or split the MMC in half, and frost each half individually (in which case you'll end up with two separate MMCs — or you can reassemble the frosted halves to create a layered MMC). Decorate, if you wish, with HERSHEY'S® semi-sweet chocolate chips or berries.

Chocolate-Covered Carrot Microwave Mug Cake

INGREDIENTS

1 egg
4 tablespoons Beech-Nut® Tender
   Sweet Carrots baby food
3 tablespoons soy milk
1 tablespoon sorghum syrup (pure sorghum)
1/8 teaspoon McCormick® vanilla extract
1/4 teaspoon Argo® baking powder
1/2 teaspoon guar gum, xantham gum, or tapioca flour
4 tablespoons Domino® light brown sugar
4 tablespoons gluten-free brown or white rice flour
4 tablespoons gluten-free sorghum flour
1 tablespoon potato starch
2 tablespoons HERSHEY'S® cocoa powder

NOTE
Thank you to the bunny who invented the chocolate-covered carrot. Who knew bunnies could be so clever?

DIRECTIONS

Prepare your microwavable mug by coating the inside lightly with cooking spray.

Mix the ingredients in a small bowl. Beat egg first with a spoon and mix in other liquid ingredients. Then add dry ingredients and mix until you've removed all the lumps.

Pour the batter into the mug (do not fill more than halfway) and smooth the top with a spoon. Thump mug firmly on the tabletop six times to remove excess air bubbles. Place mug on top of a microwavable small plate or saucer.

Bake for 3 - 4 minutes. Check for doneness by inserting a toothpick in the middle of the microwave mug cake and removing the toothpick. If the toothpick is dry, the MMC is done.

Wait 2 minutes, then run a butter knife along the inside of the mug, and tip the cake onto a plate. Position the mug cake so that the slightly rounded surface is on top. Your microwave mug cake will now look like a slightly overgrown muffin.

FANCY STUFF

Drizzle the whole Chocolate-Covered Carrot Microwave Mug Cake with Hershey's chocolate syrup, or split the MMC in half, and drizzle each half individually (in which case you'll end up with two separate MMCs — or you can reassemble the drizzled halves to create a layered MMC). Decorate, if you wish, with HERSHEY'S® semi-sweet chocolate chips.

Chocolate-Dipped Strawberry Microwave Mug Cake

INGREDIENTS
1 egg
3 tablespoons Yoplait® Strawberry yogurt
3 tablespoons milk
2 tablespoons oil
1/8 teaspoon McCormick® vanilla extract
1/4 teaspoon Argo® baking powder
1/2 teaspoon guar gum, xantham gum, or tapioca flour
1/2 teaspoon McCormick® ground cinnamon
4 tablespoons Domino® light brown sugar
4 tablespoons gluten-free soy flour
4 tablespoons gluten-free sorghum flour
1 tablespoon potato starch
2 tablespoons white chocolate JELL-O® pudding powder

NOTE
Why do strawberries always taste so much better when they've been dipped into chocolate? And, given that they do, why don't they just grow that way naturally?

DIRECTIONS
Prepare your microwavable mug by coating the inside lightly with PAM Original cooking spray.

Mix the ingredients in a small bowl. Beat egg first with a spoon and mix in other liquid ingredients. Then add dry ingredients and mix until you've removed all the lumps.

Pour the batter into the mug (do not fill more than halfway) and smooth the top with a spoon. Thump mug firmly on the tabletop six times to remove excess air bubbles. Place mug on top of a microwavable small plate or saucer.

Bake for 3 - 4 minutes. Check for doneness by inserting a toothpick in the middle of the microwave mug cake and removing the toothpick. If the toothpick is dry, the MMC is done.

Wait 2 minutes, then run a butter knife along the inside of the mug, and tip the cake onto a plate. Position the mug cake so that the slightly rounded surface is on top. Your microwave mug cake will now look like a slightly overgrown muffin.

FANCY STUFF
Drizzle the whole Chocolate-Dipped Strawberry Microwave Mug Cake with Yoplait® Strawberry yogurt or Duncan Hines® Creamy Home-Style Strawberry Cream Frosting, or split the MMC in half, and frost each half individually (in which case you'll end up with two separate MMCs — or you can reassemble the frosted halves to create a layered MMC). Decorate, if you wish, with sliced strawberries.

Chocopeach Molasses Microwave Mug Cake

INGREDIENTS
1 egg
3 tablespoons Beech-Nut® Peaches baby food
1 tablespoon Grandma's® Original Molasses
5 tablespoons rice milk
1/8 teaspoon McCormick® vanilla extract
1/4 teaspoon Argo® baking powder
1/2 teaspoon guar gum, xantham gum, or tapioca flour
1/2 teaspoon McCormick® ground ginger
1/4 teaspoon McCormick® ground cinnamon
pinch of McCormick® ground cloves
4 tablespoons Domino® light brown sugar
4 tablespoons gluten-free buckwheat flour
4 tablespoons gluten-free brown or white rice flour
1 tablespoon potato starch
1 tablespoon HERSHEY'S® cocoa powder

NOTE

Why don't most people bother to peel peaches? Probably for the same reason people don't dip the pits into chocolate.

DIRECTIONS
Prepare your microwavable mug by coating the inside lightly with PAM Original cooking spray.

Mix the ingredients in a small bowl. Beat egg first with a spoon and mix in other liquid ingredients. Then add dry ingredients and mix until you've removed all the lumps.

Pour the batter into the mug (do not fill more than halfway) and smooth the top with a spoon. Thump mug firmly on the tabletop six times to remove excess air bubbles. Place mug on top of a microwavable small plate or saucer.

Bake for 3 - 4 minutes. Check for doneness by inserting a toothpick in the middle of the microwave mug cake and removing the toothpick. If the toothpick is dry, the MMC is done.

Wait 2 minutes, then run a butter knife along the inside of the mug, and tip the cake onto a plate. Position the mug cake so that the slightly rounded surface is on top. Your microwave mug cake will now look like a slightly overgrown muffin.

FANCY STUFF
Drizzle the whole Chocopeach Molasses Microwave Mug Cake with Duncan Hines® Creamy Home-Style Classic Chocolate Frosting, or split the MMC in half, and frost each half individually (in which case you'll end up with two separate MMCs — or you can reassemble the frosted halves to create a layered MMC). Decorate, if you wish, with your choice of sliced fruit or gluten-free candies.

Coconut Cream Microwave Mug Cake

INGREDIENTS
1 egg
2 tablespoons Yoplait® French Vanilla yogurt
4 tablespoons milk
2 tablespoons oil
1/8 teaspoon McCormick® coconut extract (or McCormick® vanilla extract)
1/4 teaspoon Argo® baking powder
1/2 teaspoon guar gum, xantham gum, or tapioca flour
1/2 teaspoon McCormick® ground cinnamon
4 tablespoons Domino® light brown sugar
2 tablespoons gluten-free coconut flour
4 tablespoons gluten-free brown or white rice flour
1 tablespoon potato starch
2 tablespoons coconut JELL-O® pudding powder
2 tablespoons shredded coconut

NOTE
Ponder this: Do you cream coconut in the same way as you cream butter?

DIRECTIONS
Prepare your microwavable mug by coating the inside lightly with PAM Original cooking spray.

Mix the ingredients in a small bowl. Beat egg first with a spoon and mix in other liquid ingredients. Then add dry ingredients and mix until you've removed all the lumps.

Pour the batter into the mug (do not fill more than halfway) and smooth the top with a spoon. Thump mug firmly on the tabletop six times to remove excess air bubbles. Place mug on top of a microwavable small plate or saucer.

Bake for 3 - 4 minutes. Check for doneness by inserting a toothpick in the middle of the microwave mug cake and removing the toothpick. If the toothpick is dry, the MMC is done.

Wait 2 minutes, then run a butter knife along the inside of the mug, and tip the cake onto a plate. Position the mug cake so that the slightly rounded surface is on top. Your microwave mug cake will now look like a slightly overgrown muffin.

FANCY STUFF
Frost the whole Coconut Cream Microwave Mug Cake with Duncan Hines® Creamy Home-Style Classic Vanilla Frosting, or split the MMC in half, and frost each half individually (in which case you'll end up with two separate MMCs — or you can reassemble the frosted halves to create a layered MMC). Decorate, if you wish, with shredded coconut.

Coconut Peach Microwave Mug Cake

INGREDIENTS
1 tablespoon apple cider vinegar
1 tablespoon flaxseed meal
2 tablespoons Beech-Nut® Peaches baby food
5 tablespoons milk
2 tablespoons Yoplait® Harvest Peach yogurt
2 tablespoons oil
1/8 teaspoon McCormick® coconut extract (or McCormick® vanilla extract)
1/4 teaspoon Argo® baking powder
1/2 teaspoon guar gum, xantham gum, or tapioca flour
1/2 teaspoon McCormick® ground cinnamon
4 tablespoons Domino® light brown sugar
1 tablespoon gluten-free coconut flour
3 tablespoons gluten-free brown or white rice flour
4 tablespoons gluten-free sorghum flour
2 tablespoons potato starch
2 tablespoons shredded coconut

NOTE
Wouldn't it be peachy if coconuts grew with soft shells?

DIRECTIONS
Prepare your microwavable mug by coating the inside lightly with PAM Original cooking spray.

Mix the ingredients in a small bowl. Add flaxseed meal to liquid ingredients and beat together. Then add dry ingredients and mix until you've removed all the lumps.

Pour the batter into the mug (do not fill more than halfway) and smooth the top with a spoon. Thump mug firmly on the tabletop six times to remove excess air bubbles. Place mug on top of a microwavable small plate or saucer.

Bake for 3 - 4 minutes. Check for doneness by inserting a toothpick in the middle of the microwave mug cake and removing the toothpick. If the toothpick is dry, the MMC is done.

Wait 2 minutes, then run a butter knife along the inside of the mug, and tip the cake onto a plate. Position the mug cake so that the slightly rounded surface is on top. Your microwave mug cake will now look like a slightly overgrown muffin.

FANCY STUFF
Frost the whole Coconut Peach Microwave Mug Cake with Yoplait® Harvest Peach yogurt or Duncan Hines® Creamy Home-Style Classic Vanilla Frosting, or split the MMC in half, and frost each half individually (in which case you'll end up with two separate MMCs — or you can reassemble the frosted halves to create a layered MMC). Decorate, if you wish, with sliced peaches or shredded coconut.

Coffee Almond Microwave Mug Cake

INGREDIENTS
1 egg
1 tablespoon Yoplait® French
  Vanilla yogurt
2 tablespoons almond milk
2 tablespoons oil
1/8 teaspoon McCormick® almond
  extract (or McCormick® vanilla extract)
1/4 teaspoon Argo® baking powder
1/2 teaspoon guar gum, xantham gum, or tapioca flour
1/2 teaspoon instant coffee powder
4 tablespoons Domino® light brown sugar
3 tablespoons gluten-free sorghum flour
3 tablespoons gluten-free almond flour
3 tablespoons gluten-free all-purpose flour
2 tablespoons potato starch
2 tablespoons almond slivers

NOTE
There's something better than a
Coffee Almond Microwave Mug
Cake with a hot drink on a cold,
wintry morning. At the moment,
though, we can't remember what
it is.

DIRECTIONS
Prepare your microwavable mug by coating the inside lightly with cooking spray.

Mix the ingredients in a small bowl. Beat egg first with a spoon and mix in other liquid ingredients. Then add dry ingredients and mix until you've removed all the lumps.

Pour the batter into the mug (do not fill more than halfway) and smooth the top with a spoon. Thump mug firmly on the tabletop six times to remove excess air bubbles. Place mug on top of a microwavable small plate or saucer.

Bake for 3 - 4 minutes. Check for doneness by inserting a toothpick in the middle of the microwave mug cake and removing the toothpick. If the toothpick is dry, the MMC is done.

Wait 2 minutes, then run a butter knife along the inside of the mug, and tip the cake onto a plate. Position the mug cake so that the slightly rounded surface is on top. Your microwave mug cake will now look like a slightly overgrown muffin.

FANCY STUFF
Frost the whole Coffee Almond Microwave Mug Cake with Yoplait® French Vanilla yogurt, or split the MMC in half, and frost each half individually (in which case you'll end up with two separate MMCs — or you can reassemble the frosted halves to create a layered MMC). Decorate, if you wish, with almond slivers.

Coffee Cheesecake Microwave Mug Cake

INGREDIENTS
1 egg
2 tablespoons Yoplait® Coffee yogurt
4 tablespoons milk
2 tablespoons oil
1/8 teaspoon McCormick® vanilla extract
1/4 teaspoon Argo® baking powder
1/2 teaspoon guar gum, xantham gum, or tapioca flour
1/2 teaspoon instant coffee powder
4 tablespoons Domino® light brown sugar
4 tablespoons gluten-free fava bean flour
4 tablespoons gluten-free brown or white rice flour
1 tablespoon potato starch
2 tablespoons cheesecake JELL-O® pudding powder

NOTE
Next time you go to a deli, be sure to order a pickle and a slice of cheesecake. Just don't drip pickle juice onto your cheesecake, because that would just about wreck the cheesecake.

DIRECTIONS
Prepare your microwavable mug by coating the inside lightly with PAM Original cooking spray.

Mix the ingredients in a small bowl. Beat egg first with a spoon and mix in other liquid ingredients. Then add dry ingredients and mix until you've removed all the lumps.

Pour the batter into the mug (do not fill more than halfway) and smooth the top with a spoon. Thump mug firmly on the tabletop six times to remove excess air bubbles. Place mug on top of a microwavable small plate or saucer.

Bake for 3 - 4 minutes. Check for doneness by inserting a toothpick in the middle of the microwave mug cake and removing the toothpick. If the toothpick is dry, the MMC is done.

Wait 2 minutes, then run a butter knife along the inside of the mug, and tip the cake onto a plate. Position the mug cake so that the slightly rounded surface is on top. Your microwave mug cake will now look like a slightly overgrown muffin.

FANCY STUFF
Frost the whole Coffee Cheesecake Microwave Mug Cake with Yoplait® Coffee yogurt, or split the MMC in half, and frost each half individually (in which case you'll end up with two separate MMCs — or you can reassemble the frosted halves to create a layered MMC). Decorate, if you wish, with sliced fruit.

Coffee Coconut Microwave Mug Cake

INGREDIENTS

1 egg

2 tablespoons Yoplait® French
Vanilla yogurt

3 tablespoons rice milk

2 tablespoons oil

1/8 teaspoon McCormick® coconut extract
(or McCormick® vanilla extract)

1/4 teaspoon Argo® baking powder

1/2 teaspoon guar gum, xantham gum, or tapioca flour

1/2 teaspoon instant coffee powder

4 tablespoons Domino® light brown sugar

2 tablespoons gluten-free coconut flour

4 tablespoons gluten-free all-purpose flour

2 tablespoons potato starch

2 tablespoons shredded coconut

NOTE

We know Gilligan had coconuts on his island. Too bad he didn't also have coffee, microwave ovens, and mugs. He really would have had something there. Oh, well.

DIRECTIONS

Prepare your microwavable mug by coating the inside lightly with PAM Original cooking spray.

Mix the ingredients in a small bowl. Beat egg first with a spoon and mix in other liquid ingredients. Then add dry ingredients and mix until you've removed all the lumps.

Pour the batter into the mug (do not fill more than halfway) and smooth the top with a spoon. Thump mug firmly on the tabletop six times to remove excess air bubbles. Place mug on top of a microwavable small plate or saucer.

Bake for 3 - 4 minutes. Check for doneness by inserting a toothpick in the middle of the microwave mug cake and removing the toothpick. If the toothpick is dry, the MMC is done.

Wait 2 minutes, then run a butter knife along the inside of the mug, and tip the cake onto a plate. Position the mug cake so that the slightly rounded surface is on top. Your microwave mug cake will now look like a slightly overgrown muffin.

FANCY STUFF

Frost the whole Coffee Coconut Microwave Mug Cake with Duncan Hines® Creamy Home-Style Classic Vanilla Frosting, or split the MMC in half, and frost each half individually (in which case you'll end up with two separate MMCs — or you can reassemble the frosted halves to create a layered MMC). Decorate, if you wish, with shredded coconut.

Coffee Sorghum Microwave Mug Cake

INGREDIENTS

1 egg
2 tablespoons Yoplait® Coffee yogurt
3 tablespoons milk
2 tablespoons oil
1/8 teaspoon McCormick® vanilla extract
1/4 teaspoon Argo® baking powder
1/2 teaspoon guar gum, xantham gum, or tapioca flour
1 tablespoon sorghum syrup (pure sorghum)
1/2 teaspoon instant coffee powder
3 tablespoons gluten-free almond flour
5 tablespoons gluten-free brown or white rice flour
1 tablespoon potato starch

NOTE

Who needs fancy coffee shops when you can make better snacks in your very own microwave oven?

DIRECTIONS

Prepare your microwavable mug by coating the inside lightly with PAM Original cooking spray.

Mix the ingredients in a small bowl. Beat egg first with a spoon and mix in other liquid ingredients. Then add dry ingredients and mix until you've removed all the lumps.

Pour the batter into the mug (do not fill more than halfway) and smooth the top with a spoon. Thump mug firmly on the tabletop six times to remove excess air bubbles. Place mug on top of a microwavable small plate or saucer.

Bake for 3 - 4 minutes. Check for doneness by inserting a toothpick in the middle of the microwave mug cake and removing the toothpick. If the toothpick is dry, the MMC is done.

Wait 2 minutes, then run a butter knife along the inside of the mug, and tip the cake onto a plate. Position the mug cake so that the slightly rounded surface is on top. Your microwave mug cake will now look like a slightly overgrown muffin.

FANCY STUFF

Frost the whole Coffee Sorghum Microwave Mug Cake with sorghum syrup (pure sorghum) or Yoplait® Coffee yogurt, or split the MMC in half, and frost each half individually (in which case you'll end up with two separate MMCs — or you can reassemble the frosted halves to create a layered MMC). Decorate, if you wish, with your choice of sliced fruit or gluten-free candies.

Corn Appleberry Microwave Mug Cake

INGREDIENTS

1 egg
2 tablespoons Beech-Nut® Apples &
Blueberries baby food
2 tablespoons soy milk
2 tablespoons oil
2 tablespoons tapioca syrup
1/8 teaspoon McCormick® vanilla extract
1/4 teaspoon Argo® baking powder
1/2 teaspoon guar gum, xantham gum, or tapioca flour
1/2 teaspoon McCormick® ground ginger
1/4 teaspoon McCormick® ground cinnamon
pinch of McCormick® ground cloves
4 tablespoons gluten-free corn flour
4 tablespoons gluten-free all-purpose flour
1 tablespoon potato starch
2 tablespoons dried blueberries

NOTE
If you're ever feeling blue, think of how blueberries must feel. They're blue all the time.

DIRECTIONS

Prepare your microwavable mug by coating the inside lightly with PAM Original cooking spray.

Mix the ingredients in a small bowl. Beat egg first with a spoon and mix in other liquid ingredients. Then add dry ingredients and mix until you've removed all the lumps.

Pour the batter into the mug (do not fill more than halfway) and smooth the top with a spoon. Thump mug firmly on the tabletop six times to remove excess air bubbles. Place mug on top of a microwavable small plate or saucer.

Bake for 3 - 4 minutes. Check for doneness by inserting a toothpick in the middle of the microwave mug cake and removing the toothpick. If the toothpick is dry, the MMC is done.

Wait 2 minutes, then run a butter knife along the inside of the mug, and tip the cake onto a plate. Position the mug cake so that the slightly rounded surface is on top. Your microwave mug cake will now look like a slightly overgrown muffin.

FANCY STUFF

Frost the whole Corn Appleberry Microwave Mug Cake with tapioca syrup, or split the MMC in half, and frost each half individually (in which case you'll end up with two separate MMCs — or you can reassemble the frosted halves to create a layered MMC). Decorate, if you wish, with your choice of sliced fruit or gluten-free candies.

Corn Muffin Microwave Mug Cake

INGREDIENTS
2 eggs
1 tablespoon Yoplait® French
Vanilla yogurt
2 tablespoons oil
1/4 teaspoon McCormick® vanilla extract
1/4 teaspoon Argo® baking powder
1/2 teaspoon guar gum, xantham gum, or
tapioca flour
4 tablespoons Domino® light brown sugar
6 tablespoons gluten-free corn flour
2 tablespoons gluten-free sorghum flour
2 tablespoons potato starch

NOTE

If passing by the farm stand without stopping for freshly-picked corn left you feeling remorseful, here's a way to get over it. Bake yourself a Corn Muffin Microwave Mug Cake. It's almost as good.

DIRECTIONS
Prepare your microwavable mug by coating the inside lightly with PAM Original cooking spray.

Mix the ingredients in a small bowl. Beat egg first with a spoon and mix in other liquid ingredients. Then add dry ingredients and mix until you've removed all the lumps.

Pour the batter into the mug (do not fill more than halfway) and smooth the top with a spoon. Thump mug firmly on the tabletop six times to remove excess air bubbles. Place mug on top of a microwavable small plate or saucer.

Bake for 3 - 4 minutes. Check for doneness by inserting a toothpick in the middle of the microwave mug cake and removing the toothpick. If the toothpick is dry, the MMC is done.

Wait 2 minutes, then run a butter knife along the inside of the mug, and tip the cake onto a plate. Position the mug cake so that the slightly rounded surface is on top. Your microwave mug cake will now look like a slightly overgrown muffin.

FANCY STUFF
Spread butter on top of the Corn Muffin Microwave Mug Cake, or split the MMC in half, and top each half with butter individually (in which case you'll end up with two separate MMCs). Top with your favorite gluten-free syrup, if you'd like.

Corny Raisin Microwave Mug Cake

INGREDIENTS

1 egg
2 tablespoons Mott's® applesauce
2 tablespoons apple juice
2 tablespoons oil
2 tablespoons sorghum syrup (pure sorghum)
1/8 teaspoon McCormick® vanilla extract
1/4 teaspoon Argo® baking powder
1/2 teaspoon guar gum, xantham gum, or tapioca flour
1/2 teaspoon McCormick® ground ginger
1/4 teaspoon McCormick® ground cinnamon
pinch of McCormick® ground cloves
4 tablespoons gluten-free corn flour
4 tablespoons gluten-free all-purpose flour
2 tablespoons potato starch
2 tablespoons Sun-Maid® Natural Sun-Dried Raisins

NOTE
All raisins are pretty corny. Check it out. Ask them to tell you a joke sometime.

DIRECTIONS

Prepare your microwavable mug by coating the inside lightly with PAM Original cooking spray.

Mix the ingredients in a small bowl. Beat egg first with a spoon and mix in other liquid ingredients. Then add dry ingredients and mix until you've removed all the lumps.

Pour the batter into the mug (do not fill more than halfway) and smooth the top with a spoon. Thump mug firmly on the tabletop six times to remove excess air bubbles. Place mug on top of a microwavable small plate or saucer.

Bake for 3 - 4 minutes. Check for doneness by inserting a toothpick in the middle of the microwave mug cake and removing the toothpick. If the toothpick is dry, the MMC is done.

Wait 2 minutes, then run a butter knife along the inside of the mug, and tip the cake onto a plate. Position the mug cake so that the slightly rounded surface is on top. Your microwave mug cake will now look like a slightly overgrown muffin.

FANCY STUFF

Frost the whole Corny Raisin Microwave Mug Cake with sorghum syrup or apple sauce, or split the MMC in half, and frost each half individually (in which case you'll end up with two separate MMCs — or you can reassemble the frosted halves to create a layered MMC). Decorate, if you wish, with Sun-Maid® Natural Sun-Dried Raisins.

Double Apricot Microwave Mug Cake

INGREDIENTS

1 egg
2 tablespoons Beech-Nut® Apricots
  with Pears & Apples baby food
4 tablespoons soy milk
2 tablespoons oil
1/8 teaspoon McCormick® vanilla extract
1/4 teaspoon Argo® baking powder
1/2 teaspoon guar gum, xantham gum, or tapioca flour
1/2 teaspoon McCormick® ground cinnamon
4 tablespoons Domino® light brown sugar
4 tablespoons gluten-free amaranth flour
4 tablespoons gluten-free brown or white rice flour
1 tablespoon potato starch
2 tablespoons apricot JELL-O® gelatin powder

NOTE
Have you ever seen a set of
identical twin apricots?

DIRECTIONS

Prepare your microwavable mug by coating the inside lightly with PAM
Original cooking spray.

Mix the ingredients in a small bowl. Beat egg first with a spoon and mix
in other liquid ingredients. Then add dry ingredients and mix until you've
removed all the lumps.

Pour the batter into the mug (do not fill more than halfway) and smooth the
top with a spoon. Thump mug firmly on the tabletop six times to remove
excess air bubbles. Place mug on top of a microwavable small plate or saucer.

Bake for 3 - 4 minutes. Check for doneness by inserting a toothpick in the
middle of the microwave mug cake and removing the toothpick. If the
toothpick is dry, the MMC is done.

Wait 2 minutes, then run a butter knife along the inside of the mug, and tip
the cake onto a plate. Position the mug cake so that the slightly rounded
surface is on top. Your microwave mug cake will now look like a slightly
overgrown muffin.

FANCY STUFF

Frost the whole Double Apricot Microwave Mug Cake with Duncan Hines®
Creamy Home-Style Butter Cream Frosting, or split the MMC in half, and
frost each half individually (in which case you'll end up with two separate
MMCs — or you can reassemble the frosted halves to create a layered MMC).
Decorate, if you wish, with sliced apricots or pears.

Double Raspberry Microwave Mug Cake

INGREDIENTS
1 egg
2 tablespoons Yoplait® Red
  Raspberry yogurt
5 tablespoons milk
2 tablespoons oil
1/8 teaspoon McCormick® vanilla extract
1/4 teaspoon Argo® baking powder
1/2 teaspoon guar gum, xantham gum, or tapioca flour
1/2 teaspoon McCormick® ground ginger
1/4 teaspoon McCormick® ground cinnamon
pinch of McCormick® ground cloves
4 tablespoons Domino® light brown sugar
4 tablespoons gluten-free quinoa flour
4 tablespoons gluten-free sorghum flour
1 tablespoon potato starch
2 tablespoons raspberry JELL-O® pudding powder

NOTE
Why is it that giving someone a raspberry is usually considered disrespectful?

DIRECTIONS
Prepare your microwavable mug by coating the inside lightly with PAM Original cooking spray.

Mix the ingredients in a small bowl. Beat egg first with a spoon and mix in other liquid ingredients. Then add dry ingredients and mix until you've removed all the lumps.

Pour the batter into the mug (do not fill more than halfway) and smooth the top with a spoon. Thump mug firmly on the tabletop six times to remove excess air bubbles. Place mug on top of a microwavable small plate or saucer.

Bake for 3 - 4 minutes. Check for doneness by inserting a toothpick in the middle of the microwave mug cake and removing the toothpick. If the toothpick is dry, the MMC is done.

Wait 2 minutes, then run a butter knife along the inside of the mug, and tip the cake onto a plate. Position the mug cake so that the slightly rounded surface is on top. Your microwave mug cake will now look like a slightly overgrown muffin.

FANCY STUFF
Frost the whole Double Raspberry Microwave Mug Cake with Yoplait® Red Raspberry yogurt, or split the MMC in half, and frost each half individually (in which case you'll end up with two separate MMCs — or you can reassemble the frosted halves to create a layered MMC). Decorate, if you wish, with raspberries.

Elvis Microwave Mug Cake

INGREDIENTS
1 egg
2 tablespoons Skippy® peanut butter
3 tablespoons Yoplait® Banana
  Crème yogurt
3 tablespoons milk
2 tablespoons oil
1/8 teaspoon McCormick® vanilla extract
1/4 teaspoon Argo® baking powder
1/2 teaspoon guar gum, xantham gum, or tapioca flour
1/2 teaspoon McCormick® ground cinnamon
4 tablespoons Domino® light brown sugar
4 tablespoons gluten-free sorghum flour
4 tablespoons gluten-free millet flour
2 tablespoons potato starch

NOTE
Why does the combination of peanut butter and bananas always bring to mind a pair of blue suede shoes?

DIRECTIONS
Prepare your microwavable mug by coating the inside lightly with PAM Original cooking spray.

Mix the ingredients in a small bowl. Beat egg first with a spoon and mix in other liquid ingredients. Then add dry ingredients and mix until you've removed all the lumps.

Pour the batter into the mug (do not fill more than halfway) and smooth the top with a spoon. Thump mug firmly on the tabletop six times to remove excess air bubbles. Place mug on top of a microwavable small plate or saucer.

Bake for 3 - 4 minutes. Check for doneness by inserting a toothpick in the middle of the microwave mug cake and removing the toothpick. If the toothpick is dry, the MMC is done.

Wait 2 minutes, then run a butter knife along the inside of the mug, and tip the cake onto a plate. Position the mug cake so that the slightly rounded surface is on top. Your microwave mug cake will now look like a slightly overgrown muffin.

FANCY STUFF
Frost the whole Elvis Microwave Mug Cake with Yoplait® Banana Crème yogurt or Duncan Hines® Creamy Home-Style Butter Cream Frosting, or split the MMC in half, and frost each half individually (in which case you'll end up with two separate MMCs — or you can reassemble the frosted halves to create a layered MMC). Decorate, if you wish, with sliced bananas.

Fruit Medley Microwave Mug Cake

INGREDIENTS

1 egg

4 tablespoons Beech-Nut® Apples, Mango & Kiwi baby food

3 tablespoons rice milk

1/8 teaspoon McCormick® vanilla extract

1/4 teaspoon Argo® baking powder

1/2 teaspoon guar gum, xantham gum, or tapioca flour

1/2 teaspoon McCormick® ground cinnamon

4 tablespoons Domino® light brown sugar

4 tablespoons gluten-free sorghum flour

4 tablespoons gluten-free brown or white rice flour

1 tablespoon potato starch

NOTE
Have you ever tried to milk a grain of rice? It isn't easy, that's for sure.

DIRECTIONS

Prepare your microwavable mug by coating the inside lightly with cooking spray.

Mix the ingredients in a small bowl. Beat egg first with a spoon and mix in other liquid ingredients. Then add dry ingredients and mix until you've removed all the lumps.

Pour the batter into the mug (do not fill more than halfway) and smooth the top with a spoon. Thump mug firmly on the tabletop six times to remove excess air bubbles. Place mug on top of a microwavable small plate or saucer.

Bake for 3 - 4 minutes. Check for doneness by inserting a toothpick in the middle of the microwave mug cake and removing the toothpick. If the toothpick is dry, the MMC is done.

Wait 2 minutes, then run a butter knife along the inside of the mug, and tip the cake onto a plate. Position the mug cake so that the slightly rounded surface is on top. Your microwave mug cake will now look like a slightly overgrown muffin.

FANCY STUFF

Sprinkle Domino® light brown sugar on the whole Fruit Medley Microwave Mug Cake, or split the MMC in half, and sprinkle each half individually (in which case you'll end up with two separate MMCs — or you can reassemble the sprinkled halves to create a layered MMC). Decorate, if you wish, with sliced fruit.

Fruitilla Microwave Mug Cake

INGREDIENTS
1 egg
2 tablespoons Beech-Nut® Apricots with Pears & Apples baby food
3 tablespoons milk
2 tablespoons oil
1 tablespoon tapioca syrup
1/8 teaspoon McCormick® vanilla extract
1/4 teaspoon Argo® baking powder
1/2 teaspoon guar gum, xantham gum, or tapioca flour
1/2 teaspoon McCormick® ground cinnamon
4 tablespoons Domino® light brown sugar
4 tablespoons gluten-free brown or white rice flour
4 tablespoons gluten-free sorghum flour
1 tablespoon potato starch
2 tablespoons vanilla JELL-O® pudding powder

NOTE
It's a fruit, it's vanilla . . . it's fruitilla!

DIRECTIONS
Prepare your microwavable mug by coating the inside lightly with PAM Original cooking spray.

Mix the ingredients in a small bowl. Beat egg first with a spoon and mix in other liquid ingredients. Then add dry ingredients and mix until you've removed all the lumps.

Pour the batter into the mug (do not fill more than halfway) and smooth the top with a spoon. Thump mug firmly on the tabletop six times to remove excess air bubbles. Place mug on top of a microwavable small plate or saucer.

Bake for 3 - 4 minutes. Check for doneness by inserting a toothpick in the middle of the microwave mug cake and removing the toothpick. If the toothpick is dry, the MMC is done.

Wait 2 minutes, then run a butter knife along the inside of the mug, and tip the cake onto a plate. Position the mug cake so that the slightly rounded surface is on top. Your microwave mug cake will now look like a slightly overgrown muffin.

FANCY STUFF
Frost the whole Fruitilla Microwave Mug Cake with Duncan Hines® Creamy Home-Style Classic Vanilla Frosting, or split the MMC in half, and frost each half individually (in which case you'll end up with two separate MMCs — or you can reassemble the frosted halves to create a layered MMC). Decorate, if you wish, with sliced fruit.

Fruits 'n Nuts Microwave Mug Cake

INGREDIENTS
1 egg
4 tablespoons Beech-Nut® Apples,
   Mango & Kiwi baby food
3 tablespoons Yoplait® Pineapple yogurt
1/8 teaspoon McCormick® vanilla extract
1/4 teaspoon Argo® baking powder
1/2 teaspoon guar gum, xantham gum, or tapioca flour
1/2 teaspoon McCormick® ground cinnamon
4 tablespoons Domino® light brown sugar
4 tablespoons gluten-free sorghum flour
4 tablespoons gluten-free soy flour
1 tablespoon potato starch
2 tablespoons almond slivers

NOTE
Four out of five mangos surveyed
prefer almonds to any other nuts.

DIRECTIONS
Prepare your microwavable mug by coating the inside lightly with cooking spray.

Mix the ingredients in a small bowl. Beat egg first with a spoon and mix in other liquid ingredients. Then add dry ingredients and mix until you've removed all the lumps.

Pour the batter into the mug (do not fill more than halfway) and smooth the top with a spoon. Thump mug firmly on the tabletop six times to remove excess air bubbles. Place mug on top of a microwavable small plate or saucer.

Bake for 3 - 4 minutes. Check for doneness by inserting a toothpick in the middle of the microwave mug cake and removing the toothpick. If the toothpick is dry, the MMC is done.

Wait 2 minutes, then run a butter knife along the inside of the mug, and tip the cake onto a plate. Position the mug cake so that the slightly rounded surface is on top. Your microwave mug cake will now look like a slightly overgrown muffin.

FANCY STUFF
Frost the whole Fruits 'n Nuts Microwave Mug Cake with Yoplait® Pineapple yogurt, or split the MMC in half, and frost each half individually (in which case you'll end up with two separate MMCs — or you can reassemble the frosted halves to create a layered MMC). Decorate, if you wish, with sliced fruit.

Giant Blueberry Microwave Mug Cake

INGREDIENTS
1 egg
2 tablespoons Beech-Nut® Apples &
   Blueberries baby food
4 tablespoons soy milk
2 tablespoons oil
1/8 teaspoon McCormick® vanilla extract
1/4 teaspoon Argo® baking powder
1/2 teaspoon guar gum, xantham gum, or tapioca flour
1/2 teaspoon McCormick® ground cinnamon
4 tablespoons Domino® light brown sugar
4 tablespoons gluten-free amaranth flour
4 tablespoons gluten-free millet flour
1 tablespoon potato starch
2 tablespoons berry blue JELL-O® pudding powder

NOTE
Can giant blueberries climb beanstalks?

DIRECTIONS
Prepare your microwavable mug by coating the inside lightly with PAM Original cooking spray.

Mix the ingredients in a small bowl. Beat egg first with a spoon and mix in other liquid ingredients. Then add dry ingredients and mix until you've removed all the lumps.

Pour the batter into the mug (do not fill more than halfway) and smooth the top with a spoon. Thump mug firmly on the tabletop six times to remove excess air bubbles. Place mug on top of a microwavable small plate or saucer.

Bake for 3 - 4 minutes. Check for doneness by inserting a toothpick in the middle of the microwave mug cake and removing the toothpick. If the toothpick is dry, the MMC is done.

Wait 2 minutes, then run a butter knife along the inside of the mug, and tip the cake onto a plate. Position the mug cake so that the slightly rounded surface is on top. Your microwave mug cake will now look like a slightly overgrown muffin.

FANCY STUFF
Frost the whole Giant Blueberry Microwave Mug Cake with Duncan Hines® Creamy Home-Style Butter Cream Frosting, or split the MMC in half, and frost each half individually (in which case you'll end up with two separate MMCs — or you can reassemble the frosted halves to create a layered MMC). Decorate, if you wish, with blueberries or sliced apples.

Giant Orange Microwave Mug Cake

INGREDIENTS
1 egg
2 tablespoons Yoplait® French
  Vanilla yogurt
2 tablespoons orange juice
2 tablespoons oil
1/8 teaspoon McCormick® vanilla extract
1/4 teaspoon Argo® baking powder
1/2 teaspoon guar gum, xantham gum, or tapioca flour
1/2 teaspoon McCormick® ground cinnamon
4 tablespoons Domino® light brown sugar
4 tablespoons gluten-free white rice flour
4 tablespoons gluten-free all-purpose flour
1 tablespoon potato starch
2 tablespoons orange JELL-O® gelatin powder

NOTE

How would you defend yourself against an armed Giant Orange? Well, don't worry about it. Giant Oranges usually don't have any arms.

DIRECTIONS
Prepare your microwavable mug by coating the inside lightly with PAM Original cooking spray.

Mix the ingredients in a small bowl. Beat egg first with a spoon and mix in other liquid ingredients. Then add dry ingredients and mix until you've removed all the lumps.

Pour the batter into the mug (do not fill more than halfway) and smooth the top with a spoon. Thump mug firmly on the tabletop six times to remove excess air bubbles. Place mug on top of a microwavable small plate or saucer.

Bake for 3 - 4 minutes. Check for doneness by inserting a toothpick in the middle of the microwave mug cake and removing the toothpick. If the toothpick is dry, the MMC is done.

Wait 2 minutes, then run a butter knife along the inside of the mug, and tip the cake onto a plate. Position the mug cake so that the slightly rounded surface is on top. Your microwave mug cake will now look like a slightly overgrown muffin.

FANCY STUFF
Frost the whole Giant Orange Microwave Mug Cake with Duncan Hines® Creamy Home-Style Classic Vanilla Frosting, or split the MMC in half, and frost each half individually (in which case you'll end up with two separate MMCs — or you can reassemble the frosted halves to create a layered MMC). Decorate, if you wish, with sliced fruit.

Gilbert Grape Microwave Mug Cake

INGREDIENTS

1 egg
2 tablespoons Yoplait® French
Vanilla yogurt
2 tablespoons grape juice
2 tablespoons oil
1/8 teaspoon McCormick® vanilla extract
1/4 teaspoon Argo® baking powder
1/2 teaspoon guar gum, xantham gum, or tapioca flour
1/2 teaspoon McCormick® ground cinnamon
4 tablespoons Domino® light brown sugar
4 tablespoons gluten-free brown or white rice flour
4 tablespoons gluten-free all-purpose flour
1 tablespoon potato starch
2 tablespoons grape JELL-O® gelatin powder

NOTE

What would you do if you were suddenly attacked by a giant grape named Gilbert? Why, you'd eat it, of course.

DIRECTIONS

Prepare your microwavable mug by coating the inside lightly with PAM Original cooking spray.

Mix the ingredients in a small bowl. Beat egg first with a spoon and mix in other liquid ingredients. Then add dry ingredients and mix until you've removed all the lumps.

Pour the batter into the mug (do not fill more than halfway) and smooth the top with a spoon. Thump mug firmly on the tabletop six times to remove excess air bubbles. Place mug on top of a microwavable small plate or saucer.

Bake for 3 - 4 minutes. Check for doneness by inserting a toothpick in the middle of the microwave mug cake and removing the toothpick. If the toothpick is dry, the MMC is done.

Wait 2 minutes, then run a butter knife along the inside of the mug, and tip the cake onto a plate. Position the mug cake so that the slightly rounded surface is on top. Your microwave mug cake will now look like a slightly overgrown muffin.

FANCY STUFF

Frost the whole Gilbert Grape Microwave Mug Cake with Duncan Hines® Creamy Home-Style Classic Vanilla Frosting, or split the MMC in half, and frost each half individually (in which case you'll end up with two separate MMCs — or you can reassemble the frosted halves to create a layered MMC). Decorate, if you wish, with sliced fruit.

Gingerbread Microwave Mug Cake

INGREDIENTS

1 egg
2 tablespoons Yoplait® French
  Vanilla yogurt
2 tablespoons oil
2 tablespoons Grandma's® Original Molasses
1/8 teaspoon McCormick® vanilla extract
1/4 teaspoon Argo® baking powder
1/2 teaspoon guar gum, xantham gum, or tapioca flour
1/2 teaspoon McCormick® ground ginger
1/4 teaspoon McCormick® ground cinnamon
pinch of McCormick® ground cloves
4 tablespoons Domino® light brown sugar
4 tablespoons gluten-free sorghum flour
4 tablespoons gluten-free all-purpose flour
2 tablespoons potato starch

NOTE

Why do they call it gingerbread when you can't even turn it into a proper sandwich?

DIRECTIONS

Prepare your microwavable mug by coating the inside lightly with PAM Original cooking spray.

Mix the ingredients in a small bowl. Beat egg first with a spoon and mix in other liquid ingredients. Then add dry ingredients and mix until you've removed all the lumps.

Pour the batter into the mug (do not fill more than halfway) and smooth the top with a spoon. Thump mug firmly on the tabletop six times to remove excess air bubbles. Place mug on top of a microwavable small plate or saucer.

Bake for 3 - 4 minutes. Check for doneness by inserting a toothpick in the middle of the microwave mug cake and removing the toothpick. If the toothpick is dry, the MMC is done.

Wait 2 minutes, then run a butter knife along the inside of the mug, and tip the cake onto a plate. Position the mug cake so that the slightly rounded surface is on top. Your microwave mug cake will now look like a slightly overgrown muffin.

FANCY STUFF

Frost the whole Gingerbread Microwave Mug Cake with Grandma's® Original Molasses, or split the MMC in half, and frost each half individually (in which case you'll end up with two separate MMCs — or you can reassemble the frosted halves to create a layered MMC). Top, if you wish, with whipped cream.

Granana Microwave Mug Cake

INGREDIENTS

1 egg
2 tablespoons Beech-Nut® Chiquita®
  Bananas baby food
2 tablespoon milk
2 tablespoons oil
1/8 teaspoon McCormick® vanilla extract
1/4 teaspoon Argo® baking powder
1/2 teaspoon guar gum, xantham gum, or tapioca flour
1/2 teaspoon McCormick® ground cinnamon
4 tablespoons Domino® light brown sugar
4 tablespoons gluten-free sorghum flour
4 tablespoons gluten-free millet flour
1 tablespoon potato starch
2 tablespoons grape JELL-O® gelatin powder

NOTE
Too bad bananas can't roll as well as grapes can.

DIRECTIONS

Prepare your microwavable mug by coating the inside lightly with PAM Original cooking spray.

Mix the ingredients in a small bowl. Beat egg first with a spoon and mix in other liquid ingredients. Then add dry ingredients and mix until you've removed all the lumps.

Pour the batter into the mug (do not fill more than halfway) and smooth the top with a spoon. Thump mug firmly on the tabletop six times to remove excess air bubbles. Place mug on top of a microwavable small plate or saucer.

Bake for 3 - 4 minutes. Check for doneness by inserting a toothpick in the middle of the microwave mug cake and removing the toothpick. If the toothpick is dry, the MMC is done.

Wait 2 minutes, then run a butter knife along the inside of the mug, and tip the cake onto a plate. Position the mug cake so that the slightly rounded surface is on top. Your microwave mug cake will now look like a slightly overgrown muffin.

FANCY STUFF

Frost the whole Granana Microwave Mug Cake with Duncan Hines® Creamy Home-Style Classic Vanilla Frosting, or split the MMC in half, and frost each half individually (in which case you'll end up with two separate MMCs — or you can reassemble the frosted halves to create a layered MMC). Decorate, if you wish, with your choice of sliced fruit or gluten-free candies.

Grandma Clara's Microwave Mug Cake

INGREDIENTS
1 egg
3 tablespoons rice milk
2 tablespoons oil
1/8 teaspoon McCormick® vanilla extract
1/4 teaspoon Argo® baking powder
1/2 teaspoon guar gum, xantham gum, or tapioca flour
4 tablespoons Domino® light brown sugar
5 tablespoons gluten-free brown or white rice flour
2 tablespoons gluten-free sorghum flour
2 tablespoons HERSHEY'S® cocoa powder
2 tablespoons HERSHEY'S® semi-sweet chocolate chips

NOTE

This microwave mug cake bears the name Grandma Clara because it's simply the best there is.

DIRECTIONS
Prepare your microwavable mug by coating the inside lightly with PAM Original cooking spray.

Mix the ingredients in a small bowl. Beat egg first with a spoon and mix in other liquid ingredients. Then add dry ingredients and mix until you've removed all the lumps.

Pour the batter into the mug (do not fill more than halfway) and smooth the top with a spoon. Thump mug firmly on the tabletop six times to remove excess air bubbles. Place mug on top of a microwavable small plate or saucer.

Bake for 3 - 4 minutes. Check for doneness by inserting a toothpick in the middle of the microwave mug cake and removing the toothpick. If the toothpick is dry, the MMC is done.

Wait 2 minutes, then run a butter knife along the inside of the mug, and tip the cake onto a plate. Position the mug cake so that the slightly rounded surface is on top. Your microwave mug cake will now look like a slightly overgrown muffin.

FANCY STUFF
Frost the whole Grandma Clara's Microwave Mug Cake with Duncan Hines® Creamy Home-Style Classic Chocolate Frosting, or split the MMC in half, and frost each half individually (in which case you'll end up with two separate MMCs — or you can reassemble the frosted halves to create a layered MMC). Decorate, if you wish, with HERSHEY'S® semi-sweet chocolate chips.

Lemon and Lime Microwave Mug Cake

INGREDIENTS
1 egg
2 tablespoons Yoplait® Lemon
  Burst yogurt
5 tablespoons milk
2 tablespoons oil
1/8 teaspoon McCormick® vanilla extract
1/4 teaspoon Argo® baking powder
1/2 teaspoon guar gum, xantham gum, or tapioca flour
1/2 teaspoon McCormick® ground cinnamon
4 tablespoons Domino® light brown sugar
4 tablespoons gluten-free buckwheat flour
4 tablespoons gluten-free sorghum flour
1 tablespoon potato starch
2 tablespoons lime JELL-O® gelatin powder

NOTE
Wouldn't it be great if you could grow a lemon yogurt tree in your own backyard?

DIRECTIONS
Prepare your microwavable mug by coating the inside lightly with PAM Original cooking spray.

Mix the ingredients in a small bowl. Beat egg first with a spoon and mix in other liquid ingredients. Then add dry ingredients and mix until you've removed all the lumps.

Pour the batter into the mug (do not fill more than halfway) and smooth the top with a spoon. Thump mug firmly on the tabletop six times to remove excess air bubbles. Place mug on top of a microwavable small plate or saucer.

Bake for 3 - 4 minutes. Check for doneness by inserting a toothpick in the middle of the microwave mug cake and removing the toothpick. If the toothpick is dry, the MMC is done.

Wait 2 minutes, then run a butter knife along the inside of the mug, and tip the cake onto a plate. Position the mug cake so that the slightly rounded surface is on top. Your microwave mug cake will now look like a slightly overgrown muffin.

FANCY STUFF
Frost the whole Lemon and Lime Microwave Mug Cake with Yoplait® Lemon Burst yogurt or Duncan Hines® Creamy Home-Style Lemon Supreme Frosting, or split the MMC in half, and frost each half individually (in which case you'll end up with two separate MMCs — or you can reassemble the frosted halves to create a layered MMC). Decorate, if you wish, with your choice of sliced fruit or gluten-free candies.

Lemon Coconut Microwave Mug Cake

INGREDIENTS
1 egg
2 tablespoons Yoplait® Lemon
  Burst yogurt
3 tablespoons soy milk
2 tablespoons oil
1/8 teaspoon McCormick® lemon or
  coconut extract (or McCormick® vanilla extract)
1/4 teaspoon Argo® baking powder
1/2 teaspoon guar gum, xantham gum, or tapioca flour
1/2 teaspoon McCormick® ground cinnamon
4 tablespoons Domino® light brown sugar
2 tablespoons gluten-free coconut flour
4 tablespoons gluten-free brown or white rice flour
1 tablespoon potato starch
2 tablespoons lemon JELL-O® pudding powder
2 tablespoons shredded coconut

NOTE
The only negative thing about a lemon tree is that you'll never find coconuts growing on it.

DIRECTIONS
Prepare your microwavable mug by coating the inside lightly with PAM Original cooking spray.

Mix the ingredients in a small bowl. Beat egg first with a spoon and mix in other liquid ingredients. Then add dry ingredients and mix until you've removed all the lumps.

Pour the batter into the mug (do not fill more than halfway) and smooth the top with a spoon. Thump mug firmly on the tabletop six times to remove excess air bubbles. Place mug on top of a microwavable small plate or saucer.

Bake for 3 - 4 minutes. Check for doneness by inserting a toothpick in the middle of the microwave mug cake and removing the toothpick. If the toothpick is dry, the MMC is done.

Wait 2 minutes, then run a butter knife along the inside of the mug, and tip the cake onto a plate. Position the mug cake so that the slightly rounded surface is on top. Your microwave mug cake will now look like a slightly overgrown muffin.

FANCY STUFF
Frost the whole Lemon Coconut Microwave Mug Cake with Yoplait® Lemon Burst yogurt, or split the MMC in half, and frost each half individually (in which case you'll end up with two separate MMCs — or you can reassemble the frosted halves to create a layered MMC). Decorate, if you wish, with shredded coconut.

Lemon Pear Microwave Mug Cake

INGREDIENTS
1 egg
2 tablespoons Beech-Nut® Pears baby food
4 tablespoons milk
2 tablespoons oil
1/8 teaspoon McCormick® vanilla extract
1/4 teaspoon Argo® baking powder
1/2 teaspoon guar gum, xantham gum, or tapioca flour
1/2 teaspoon McCormick® ground cinnamon
4 tablespoons Domino® light brown sugar
4 tablespoons gluten-free fava bean flour
4 tablespoons gluten-free brown or white rice flour
1 tablespoon potato starch
2 tablespoons lemon JELL-O® pudding powder

NOTE
Any time you can eat a lemon, it's a pear-y good day, indeed.

DIRECTIONS
Prepare your microwavable mug by coating the inside lightly with PAM Original cooking spray.

Mix the ingredients in a small bowl. Beat egg first with a spoon and mix in other liquid ingredients. Then add dry ingredients and mix until you've removed all the lumps.

Pour the batter into the mug (do not fill more than halfway) and smooth the top with a spoon. Thump mug firmly on the tabletop six times to remove excess air bubbles. Place mug on top of a microwavable small plate or saucer.

Bake for 3 - 4 minutes. Check for doneness by inserting a toothpick in the middle of the microwave mug cake and removing the toothpick. If the toothpick is dry, the MMC is done.

Wait 2 minutes, then run a butter knife along the inside of the mug, and tip the cake onto a plate. Position the mug cake so that the slightly rounded surface is on top. Your microwave mug cake will now look like a slightly overgrown muffin.

FANCY STUFF
Frost the whole Lemon Pear Microwave Mug Cake with Duncan Hines® Creamy Home-Style Classic Vanilla Frosting, or split the MMC in half, and frost each half individually (in which case you'll end up with two separate MMCs — or you can reassemble the frosted halves to create a layered MMC). Decorate, if you wish, with sliced pears.

Lemon Tree Microwave Mug Cake

INGREDIENTS
1 egg
2 tablespoons Yoplait® Lemon Burst yogurt
5 tablespoons milk
2 tablespoons oil
1/8 teaspoon McCormick® vanilla extract
1/4 teaspoon Argo® baking powder
1/2 teaspoon guar gum, xantham gum, or tapioca flour
1/2 teaspoon McCormick® ground cinnamon
4 tablespoons Domino® light brown sugar
4 tablespoons gluten-free buckwheat flour
4 tablespoons gluten-free sorghum flour
1 tablespoon potato starch
2 tablespoons lemon JELL-O® pudding powder

NOTE
Why does the phrase "lemon tree" always make a person feel like singing?

DIRECTIONS
Prepare your microwavable mug by coating the inside lightly with PAM Original cooking spray.

Mix the ingredients in a small bowl. Beat egg first with a spoon and mix in other liquid ingredients. Then add dry ingredients and mix until you've removed all the lumps.

Pour the batter into the mug (do not fill more than halfway) and smooth the top with a spoon. Thump mug firmly on the tabletop six times to remove excess air bubbles. Place mug on top of a microwavable small plate or saucer.

Bake for 3 - 4 minutes. Check for doneness by inserting a toothpick in the middle of the microwave mug cake and removing the toothpick. If the toothpick is dry, the MMC is done.

Wait 2 minutes, then run a butter knife along the inside of the mug, and tip the cake onto a plate. Position the mug cake so that the slightly rounded surface is on top. Your microwave mug cake will now look like a slightly overgrown muffin.

FANCY STUFF
Frost the whole Lemon Tree Microwave Mug Cake with Yoplait® Lemon Burst yogurt or Duncan Hines® Creamy Home-Style Lemon Supreme Frosting, or split the MMC in half, and frost each half individually (in which case you'll end up with two separate MMCs — or you can reassemble the frosted halves to create a layered MMC). Decorate, if you wish, with sliced fruit.

Lemony Microwave Mug Cake

INGREDIENTS

1 tablespoon apple cider vinegar
1 tablespoon flaxseed meal plus 2
   tablespoons cold water
2 tablespoons Yoplait® Lemon Burst yogurt
1 tablespoon milk
2 tablespoons lemon juice
2 tablespoons oil
1/8 teaspoon McCormick® vanilla extract
1/4 teaspoon Argo® baking powder
1/2 teaspoon guar gum, xantham gum, or tapioca flour
1/2 teaspoon McCormick® ground cinnamon
4 tablespoons Domino® light brown sugar
4 tablespoons gluten-free sorghum flour
4 tablespoons gluten-free millet flour
2 tablespoons potato starch

NOTE

If you're lucky enough to live in a lovely climate where you can reach out and pick a fresh lemon nearly any month of the year, please pick one for the rest of us!

DIRECTIONS

Prepare your microwavable mug by coating the inside lightly with PAM Original cooking spray.

Mix the ingredients in a small bowl. Add flaxseed meal to liquid ingredients and beat together. Then add dry ingredients and mix until you've removed all the lumps.

Pour the batter into the mug (do not fill more than halfway) and smooth the top with a spoon. Thump mug firmly on the tabletop six times to remove excess air bubbles. Place mug on top of a microwavable small plate or saucer.

Bake for 3 - 4 minutes. Check for doneness by inserting a toothpick in the middle of the microwave mug cake and removing the toothpick. If the toothpick is dry, the MMC is done.

Wait 2 minutes, then run a butter knife along the inside of the mug, and tip the cake onto a plate. Position the mug cake so that the slightly rounded surface is on top. Your microwave mug cake will now look like a slightly overgrown muffin.

FANCY STUFF

Frost the whole Lemony Microwave Mug Cake with Yoplait® Lemon Burst yogurt, or split the MMC in half, and frost each half individually (in which case you'll end up with two separate MMCs — or you can reassemble the frosted halves to create a layered MMC). Decorate, if you wish, with sliced fruit.

Lime Coconut Microwave Mug Cake

INGREDIENTS
1 egg
2 tablespoons Yoplait® French
  Vanilla yogurt
3 tablespoons milk
2 tablespoons oil
1/8 teaspoon McCormick® coconut extract
  (or McCormick® vanilla extract)
1/4 teaspoon Argo® baking powder
1/2 teaspoon guar gum, xantham gum, or tapioca flour
1/2 teaspoon McCormick® ground cinnamon
4 tablespoons Domino® light brown sugar
2 tablespoons gluten-free coconut flour
4 tablespoons gluten-free brown or white rice flour
1 tablespoon potato starch
2 tablespoons lime JELL-O® gelatin powder
2 tablespoons shredded coconut

NOTE
Ever wonder what would happen
if you really put the lime in the
coconut, the way the song says?
Come on. You know you did.

DIRECTIONS
Prepare your microwavable mug by coating the inside lightly with PAM Original cooking spray.

Mix the ingredients in a small bowl. Beat egg first with a spoon and mix in other liquid ingredients. Then add dry ingredients and mix until you've removed all the lumps.

Pour the batter into the mug (do not fill more than halfway) and smooth the top with a spoon. Thump mug firmly on the tabletop six times to remove excess air bubbles. Place mug on top of a microwavable small plate or saucer.

Bake for 3 - 4 minutes. Check for doneness by inserting a toothpick in the middle of the microwave mug cake and removing the toothpick. If the toothpick is dry, the MMC is done.

Wait 2 minutes, then run a butter knife along the inside of the mug, and tip the cake onto a plate. Position the mug cake so that the slightly rounded surface is on top. Your microwave mug cake will now look like a slightly overgrown muffin.

FANCY STUFF
Frost the whole Lime Coconut Microwave Mug Cake with Duncan Hines® Creamy Home-Style Classic Vanilla Frosting, or split the MMC in half, and frost each half individually (in which case you'll end up with two separate MMCs — or you can reassemble the frosted halves to create a layered MMC). Decorate, if you wish, with shredded coconut.

Mango Apricot Microwave Mug Cake

INGREDIENTS

1 egg
2 tablespoons Beech-Nut® Mango baby food
2 tablespoons soy milk
2 tablespoons oil
1/8 teaspoon McCormick® vanilla extract
1/4 teaspoon Argo® baking powder
1/2 teaspoon guar gum, xantham gum, or tapioca flour
1/2 teaspoon McCormick® ground cinnamon
4 tablespoons Domino® light brown sugar
4 tablespoons gluten-free brown or white rice flour
4 tablespoons gluten-free all-purpose flour
1 tablespoon potato starch
2 tablespoons apricot JELL-O® gelatin powder

NOTE
Who decided that mangos and apricots have pits and not seeds? Really? Who decides these things?

DIRECTIONS

Prepare your microwavable mug by coating the inside lightly with PAM Original cooking spray.

Mix the ingredients in a small bowl. Beat egg first with a spoon and mix in other liquid ingredients. Then add dry ingredients and mix until you've removed all the lumps.

Pour the batter into the mug (do not fill more than halfway) and smooth the top with a spoon. Thump mug firmly on the tabletop six times to remove excess air bubbles. Place mug on top of a microwavable small plate or saucer.

Bake for 3 - 4 minutes. Check for doneness by inserting a toothpick in the middle of the microwave mug cake and removing the toothpick. If the toothpick is dry, the MMC is done.

Wait 2 minutes, then run a butter knife along the inside of the mug, and tip the cake onto a plate. Position the mug cake so that the slightly rounded surface is on top. Your microwave mug cake will now look like a slightly overgrown muffin.

FANCY STUFF

Frost the whole Mango Apricot Microwave Mug Cake with Duncan Hines® Creamy Home-Style Classic Vanilla Frosting, or split the MMC in half, and frost each half individually (in which case you'll end up with two separate MMCs — or you can reassemble the frosted halves to create a layered MMC). Decorate, if you wish, with your choice of sliced fruit or gluten-free candies.

Mixed Fruit Rice Pudding Microwave Mug Cake

INGREDIENTS
1 egg
2 tablespoons Beech-Nut® Apples,
   Mango & Kiwi baby food
2 tablespoons rice milk
2 tablespoons oil
1/8 teaspoon McCormick® vanilla extract
1/4 teaspoon Argo® baking powder
1/2 teaspoon guar gum, xantham gum, or tapioca flour
1/2 teaspoon McCormick® ground cinnamon
4 tablespoons Domino® light brown sugar
4 tablespoons gluten-free brown or white rice flour
4 tablespoons gluten-free millet flour
2 tablespoons potato starch
1 tablespoon leftover prepared Minute® rice

NOTE
Close your eyes for a moment and imagine that rice pudding grew on bushes the way that blueberries do. Okay. You can open your eyes now.

DIRECTIONS
Prepare your microwavable mug by coating the inside lightly with PAM Original cooking spray.

Mix the ingredients in a small bowl. Beat egg first with a spoon and mix in other liquid ingredients. Then add dry ingredients and mix until you've removed all the lumps.

Pour the batter into the mug (do not fill more than halfway) and smooth the top with a spoon. Thump mug firmly on the tabletop six times to remove excess air bubbles. Place mug on top of a microwavable small plate or saucer.

Bake for 3 - 4 minutes. Check for doneness by inserting a toothpick in the middle of the microwave mug cake and removing the toothpick. If the toothpick is dry, the MMC is done.

Wait 2 minutes, then run a butter knife along the inside of the mug, and tip the cake onto a plate. Position the mug cake so that the slightly rounded surface is on top. Your microwave mug cake will now look like a slightly overgrown muffin.

FANCY STUFF
Frost the whole Mixed Fruit Rice Pudding Microwave Mug Cake with Duncan Hines® Creamy Home-Style Classic Vanilla Frosting or split the MMC in half, and frost each half individually (in which case you'll end up with two separate MMCs — or you can reassemble the frosted halves to create a layered MMC). Decorate, if you wish, with sliced fruit.

Mocha Microwave Mug Cake

INGREDIENTS
1 egg
2 tablespoons Yoplait® Coffee yogurt
4 tablespoons milk
2 tablespoons oil
1/8 teaspoon McCormick® vanilla extract
1/4 teaspoon Argo® baking powder
1/2 teaspoon guar gum, xantham gum, or tapioca flour
1/2 teaspoon McCormick® ground cinnamon
4 tablespoons Domino® light brown sugar
4 tablespoons gluten-free amaranth flour
4 tablespoons gluten-free sorghum flour
1 tablespoon potato starch
2 tablespoons HERSHEY'S® cocoa powder

NOTE
Why isn't the combination of coffee and chocolate called choffee or cofflate instead of mocha?

DIRECTIONS
Prepare your microwavable mug by coating the inside lightly with PAM Original cooking spray.

Mix the ingredients in a small bowl. Beat egg first with a spoon and mix in other liquid ingredients. Then add dry ingredients and mix until you've removed all the lumps.

Pour the batter into the mug (do not fill more than halfway) and smooth the top with a spoon. Thump mug firmly on the tabletop six times to remove excess air bubbles. Place mug on top of a microwavable small plate or saucer.

Bake for 3 - 4 minutes. Check for doneness by inserting a toothpick in the middle of the microwave mug cake and removing the toothpick. If the toothpick is dry, the MMC is done.

Wait 2 minutes, then run a butter knife along the inside of the mug, and tip the cake onto a plate. Position the mug cake so that the slightly rounded surface is on top. Your microwave mug cake will now look like a slightly overgrown muffin.

FANCY STUFF
Frost the whole Mocha Microwave Mug Cake with Yoplait® Coffee yogurt or Duncan Hines® Creamy Home-Style Milk Chocolate Frosting, or split the MMC in half, and frost each half individually (in which case you'll end up with two separate MMCs — or you can reassemble the frosted halves to create a layered MMC). Decorate, if you wish, with HERSHEY'S® semi-sweet chocolate chips.

Molasses Pudding Microwave Mug Cake

INGREDIENTS

1 egg
1 tablespoon canned pumpkin
2 tablespoons Grandma's®
  Original Molasses
1 tablespoon soy milk
2 tablespoons oil
1/8 teaspoon McCormick® vanilla extract
1/4 teaspoon Argo® baking powder
1/2 teaspoon guar gum, xantham gum, or tapioca flour
1/2 teaspoon McCormick® ground ginger
1/4 teaspoon McCormick® ground cinnamon
pinch of McCormick® ground cloves
5 tablespoons gluten-free sorghum flour
3 tablespoons gluten-free corn flour
2 tablespoons potato starch
2 tablespoons Sun-Maid® Natural Sun-Dried Raisins

NOTE

Why do so many people wait for Thanksgiving to indulge in molasses pudding? Who knows? Just be grateful you don't have to be one of them.

DIRECTIONS

Prepare your microwavable mug by coating the inside lightly with PAM Original cooking spray.

Mix the ingredients in a small bowl. Beat egg first with a spoon and mix in other liquid ingredients. Then add dry ingredients and mix until you've removed all the lumps.

Pour the batter into the mug (do not fill more than halfway) and smooth the top with a spoon. Thump mug firmly on the tabletop six times to remove excess air bubbles. Place mug on top of a microwavable small plate or saucer.

Bake for 3 - 4 minutes. Check for doneness by inserting a toothpick in the middle of the microwave mug cake and removing the toothpick. If the toothpick is dry, the MMC is done.

Wait 2 minutes, then run a butter knife along the inside of the mug, and tip the cake onto a plate. Position the mug cake so that the slightly rounded surface is on top. Your microwave mug cake will now look like a slightly overgrown muffin.

FANCY STUFF

Frost the whole Molasses Pudding Microwave Mug Cake with whipped cream, or split the MMC in half, and frost each half individually (in which case you'll end up with two separate MMCs — or you can reassemble the frosted halves to create a layered MMC). Decorate, if you wish, with Sun-Maid® Natural Sun-Dried Raisins.

Molasses Rice Pudding Microwave Mug Cake

INGREDIENTS
1 egg
1 tablespoon Grandma's®
  Original Molasses
3 tablespoons rice milk
2 tablespoons oil
1/8 teaspoon McCormick® vanilla extract
1/4 teaspoon Argo® baking powder
1/2 teaspoon guar gum, xantham gum, or tapioca flour
1/2 teaspoon McCormick® ground cinnamon
4 tablespoons Domino® light brown sugar
4 tablespoons gluten-free brown or white rice flour
4 tablespoons gluten-free sorghum flour
2 tablespoons vanilla JELL-O® pudding powder
1 tablespoon leftover prepared Minute® rice
1 tablespoon Sun-Maid® Natural Sun-Dried Raisins

NOTE
Hold your tongue and say "Molasses Rice Pudding Microwave Mug Cake is on the table." Nothing much happens, does it?

DIRECTIONS
Prepare your microwavable mug by coating the inside lightly with PAM Original cooking spray.

Mix the ingredients in a small bowl. Beat egg first with a spoon and mix in other liquid ingredients. Then add dry ingredients and mix until you've removed all the lumps.

Pour the batter into the mug (do not fill more than halfway) and smooth the top with a spoon. Thump mug firmly on the tabletop six times to remove excess air bubbles. Place mug on top of a microwavable small plate or saucer.

Bake for 3 - 4 minutes. Check for doneness by inserting a toothpick in the middle of the microwave mug cake and removing the toothpick. If the toothpick is dry, the MMC is done.

Wait 2 minutes, then run a butter knife along the inside of the mug, and tip the cake onto a plate. Position the mug cake so that the slightly rounded surface is on top. Your microwave mug cake will now look like a slightly overgrown muffin.

FANCY STUFF
Frost the whole Molasses Rice Pudding Microwave Mug Cake with whipped cream, or split the MMC in half, and frost each half individually (in which case you'll end up with two separate MMCs — or you can reassemble the frosted halves to create a layered MMC). Decorate, if you wish, with Sun-Maid® Natural Sun-Dried Raisins.

Orange Apple Microwave Mug Cake

INGREDIENTS

1 egg
2 tablespoons Mott's® applesauce
2 tablespoons orange juice
2 tablespoons oil
1/8 teaspoon McCormick® vanilla extract
1/4 teaspoon Argo® baking powder
1/2 teaspoon guar gum, xantham gum, or tapioca flour
1/2 teaspoon McCormick® ground cinnamon
4 tablespoons Domino® light brown sugar
4 tablespoons gluten-free sorghum flour
4 tablespoons gluten-free millet flour
2 tablespoons potato starch

NOTE

The Orange Apple Microwave Mug Cake raises the age-old question: how can you compare oranges to apples?

DIRECTIONS

Prepare your microwavable mug by coating the inside lightly with PAM Original cooking spray.

Mix the ingredients in a small bowl. Beat egg first with a spoon and mix in other liquid ingredients. Then add dry ingredients and mix until you've removed all the lumps.

Pour the batter into the mug (do not fill more than halfway) and smooth the top with a spoon. Thump mug firmly on the tabletop six times to remove excess air bubbles. Place mug on top of a microwavable small plate or saucer.

Bake for 3 - 4 minutes. Check for doneness by inserting a toothpick in the middle of the microwave mug cake and removing the toothpick. If the toothpick is dry, the MMC is done.

Wait 2 minutes, then run a butter knife along the inside of the mug, and tip the cake onto a plate. Position the mug cake so that the slightly rounded surface is on top. Your microwave mug cake will now look like a slightly overgrown muffin.

FANCY STUFF

Frost the whole Orange Apple Microwave Mug Cake with Duncan Hines® Creamy Home-Style Classic Vanilla Frosting, or split the MMC in half, and frost each half individually (in which case you'll end up with two separate MMCs — or you can reassemble the frosted halves to create a layered MMC). Decorate, if you wish, with apple slices.

Orange Coconut Microwave Mug Cake

INGREDIENTS

1 egg
4 tablespoons orange juice
2 tablespoons oil
1/8 teaspoon McCormick® coconut extract (or McCormick® vanilla extract)
1/4 teaspoon Argo® baking powder
1/2 teaspoon guar gum, xantham gum, or tapioca flour
1/2 teaspoon McCormick® ground ginger
4 tablespoons Domino® light brown sugar
4 tablespoons gluten-free sorghum flour
4 tablespoons gluten-free brown or white rice flour
2 tablespoons potato starch
2 tablespoons shredded coconut

NOTE
What do you get if you cross an orange and a coconut? I don't know, but it's probably a better idea to try to get along with oranges and coconuts than to cross them, anyway.

DIRECTIONS

Prepare your microwavable mug by coating the inside lightly with cooking spray.

Mix the ingredients in a small bowl. Beat egg first with a spoon and mix in other liquid ingredients. Then add dry ingredients and mix until you've removed all the lumps.

Pour the batter into the mug (do not fill more than halfway) and smooth the top with a spoon. Thump mug firmly on the tabletop six times to remove excess air bubbles. Place mug on top of a microwavable small plate or saucer.

Bake for 3 - 4 minutes. Check for doneness by inserting a toothpick in the middle of the microwave mug cake and removing the toothpick. If the toothpick is dry, the MMC is done.

Wait 2 minutes, then run a butter knife along the inside of the mug, and tip the cake onto a plate. Position the mug cake so that the slightly rounded surface is on top. Your microwave mug cake will now look like a slightly overgrown muffin.

FANCY STUFF

Frost the whole Orange Coconut Microwave Mug Cake with Duncan Hines® Creamy Home-Style Classic Vanilla Frosting, or split the MMC in half, and frost each half individually (in which case you'll end up with two separate MMCs — or you can reassemble the frosted halves to create a layered MMC). Decorate, if you wish, with shredded coconut.

Orange Grove Microwave Mug Cake

INGREDIENTS
1 egg
2 tablespoons Yoplait® Orange
  Crème yogurt
5 tablespoons milk
2 tablespoons oil
1/8 teaspoon McCormick® vanilla extract
1/4 teaspoon Argo® baking powder
1/2 teaspoon guar gum, xantham gum, or tapioca flour
1/2 teaspoon McCormick® ground cinnamon
4 tablespoons Domino® light brown sugar
4 tablespoons gluten-free buckwheat flour
4 tablespoons gluten-free sorghum flour
1 tablespoon potato starch
2 tablespoons orange JELL-O® gelatin powder

NOTE
Why hasn't someone invented an
orange peeling machine?

DIRECTIONS
Prepare your microwavable mug by coating the inside lightly with PAM Original cooking spray.

Mix the ingredients in a small bowl. Beat egg first with a spoon and mix in other liquid ingredients. Then add dry ingredients and mix until you've removed all the lumps.

Pour the batter into the mug (do not fill more than halfway) and smooth the top with a spoon. Thump mug firmly on the tabletop six times to remove excess air bubbles. Place mug on top of a microwavable small plate or saucer.

Bake for 3 - 4 minutes. Check for doneness by inserting a toothpick in the middle of the microwave mug cake and removing the toothpick. If the toothpick is dry, the MMC is done.

Wait 2 minutes, then run a butter knife along the inside of the mug, and tip the cake onto a plate. Position the mug cake so that the slightly rounded surface is on top. Your microwave mug cake will now look like a slightly overgrown muffin.

FANCY STUFF
Frost the whole Orange Grove Microwave Mug Cake with Yoplait® Orange Crème yogurt or Duncan Hines® Creamy Home-Style Classic Vanilla Frosting, or split the MMC in half, and frost each half individually (in which case you'll end up with two separate MMCs — or you can reassemble the frosted halves to create a layered MMC). Decorate, if you wish, with your choice of sliced fruit or gluten-free candies.

Orange Mango Microwave Mug Cake

INGREDIENTS

1 egg
2 tablespoons Beech-Nut® Mango baby food
2 tablespoons orange juice
2 tablespoons oil
1/8 teaspoon McCormick® vanilla extract
1/4 teaspoon Argo® baking powder
1/2 teaspoon guar gum, xantham gum, or tapioca flour
1/2 teaspoon McCormick® ground cinnamon
4 tablespoons Domino® light brown sugar
3 tablespoons gluten-free almond flour
3 tablespoons gluten-free all-purpose flour
2 tablespoons gluten-free sorghum flour
2 tablespoons potato starch

NOTE

When you're slicing a mango, remember to stop when you get to the pit. Otherwise, you might dent your knife.

DIRECTIONS

Prepare your microwavable mug by coating the inside lightly with cooking spray.

Mix the ingredients in a small bowl. Beat egg first with a spoon and mix in other liquid ingredients. Then add dry ingredients and mix until you've removed all the lumps.

Pour the batter into the mug (do not fill more than halfway) and smooth the top with a spoon. Thump mug firmly on the tabletop six times to remove excess air bubbles. Place mug on top of a microwavable small plate or saucer.

Bake for 3 - 4 minutes. Check for doneness by inserting a toothpick in the middle of the microwave mug cake and removing the toothpick. If the toothpick is dry, the MMC is done.

Wait 2 minutes, then run a butter knife along the inside of the mug, and tip the cake onto a plate. Position the mug cake so that the slightly rounded surface is on top. Your microwave mug cake will now look like a slightly overgrown muffin.

FANCY STUFF

Frost the whole Orange Mango Microwave Mug Cake with Duncan Hines® Creamy Home-Style Classic Vanilla Frosting, or split the MMC in half, and frost each half individually (in which case you'll end up with two separate MMCs — or you can reassemble the frosted halves to create a layered MMC). Decorate, if you wish, with sliced mangoes.

Peach Almond Microwave Mug Cake

INGREDIENTS
1 egg
2 tablespoons Yoplait® Harvest
   Peach yogurt
2 tablespoons milk
2 tablespoons oil
1/8 teaspoon McCormick® almond
   extract (or McCormick® vanilla extract)
1/4 teaspoon Argo® baking powder
1/2 teaspoon guar gum, xantham gum, or tapioca flour
1/2 teaspoon McCormick® ground cinnamon
4 tablespoons Domino® light brown sugar
3 tablespoons gluten-free almond flour
3 tablespoons gluten-free all-purpose flour
2 tablespoons gluten-free sorghum flour
2 tablespoons potato starch
2 tablespoons almond slivers

NOTE
If you can't be either a peach or an almond, then you should at least try to taste like one. Or you can try to look like one, instead, but that wouldn't be nearly as good.

DIRECTIONS
Prepare your microwavable mug by coating the inside lightly with cooking spray.

Mix the ingredients in a small bowl. Beat egg first with a spoon and mix in other liquid ingredients. Then add dry ingredients and mix until you've removed all the lumps.

Pour the batter into the mug (do not fill more than halfway) and smooth the top with a spoon. Thump mug firmly on the tabletop six times to remove excess air bubbles. Place mug on top of a microwavable small plate or saucer.

Bake for 3 - 4 minutes. Check for doneness by inserting a toothpick in the middle of the microwave mug cake and removing the toothpick. If the toothpick is dry, the MMC is done.

Wait 2 minutes, then run a butter knife along the inside of the mug, and tip the cake onto a plate. Position the mug cake so that the slightly rounded surface is on top. Your microwave mug cake will now look like a slightly overgrown muffin.

FANCY STUFF
Frost the whole Peach Almond Microwave Mug Cake with Yoplait® Harvest Peach yogurt, or split the MMC in half, and frost each half individually (in which case you'll end up with two separate MMCs — or you can reassemble the frosted halves to create a layered MMC). Decorate, if you wish, with sliced peaches or almond silvers.

Peach Sorghum Microwave Mug Cake

INGREDIENTS

1 egg
2 tablespoons Beech-Nut® Peaches baby food
3 tablespoons rice milk
2 tablespoons oil
1/8 teaspoon McCormick® vanilla extract
1/4 teaspoon Argo® baking powder
1/2 teaspoon guar gum, xantham gum, or tapioca flour
1 tablespoon sorghum syrup (pure sorghum)
1/2 teaspoon McCormick® ground ginger
1/4 teaspoon McCormick® ground cinnamon
pinch of McCormick® ground cloves
3 tablespoons gluten-free almond flour
5 tablespoons gluten-free brown or white rice flour
1 tablespoon potato starch

NOTE
Have you ever actually seen a perfect peach? We haven't, either, but we sure like the alliteration.

DIRECTIONS

Prepare your microwavable mug by coating the inside lightly with PAM Original cooking spray.

Mix the ingredients in a small bowl. Beat egg first with a spoon and mix in other liquid ingredients. Then add dry ingredients and mix until you've removed all the lumps.

Pour the batter into the mug (do not fill more than halfway) and smooth the top with a spoon. Thump mug firmly on the tabletop six times to remove excess air bubbles. Place mug on top of a microwavable small plate or saucer.

Bake for 3 - 4 minutes. Check for doneness by inserting a toothpick in the middle of the microwave mug cake and removing the toothpick. If the toothpick is dry, the MMC is done.

Wait 2 minutes, then run a butter knife along the inside of the mug, and tip the cake onto a plate. Position the mug cake so that the slightly rounded surface is on top. Your microwave mug cake will now look like a slightly overgrown muffin.

FANCY STUFF

Frost the whole Peach Sorghum Microwave Mug Cake with sorghum syrup (pure sorghum), or split the MMC in half, and frost each half individually (in which case you'll end up with two separate MMCs — or you can reassemble the frosted halves to create a layered MMC). Decorate, if you wish, with sliced peaches.

Peachilla Microwave Mug Cake

INGREDIENTS
1 egg
3 tablespoons Beech-Nut® Peaches
  baby food
2 tablespoons Yoplait® French
  Vanilla yogurt
1 tablespoon milk
2 tablespoons oil
1/8 teaspoon McCormick® vanilla extract
1/4 teaspoon Argo® baking powder
1/2 teaspoon guar gum, xantham gum, or tapioca flour
1/2 teaspoon McCormick® ground cinnamon
4 tablespoons Domino® light brown sugar
4 tablespoons gluten-free sorghum flour
4 tablespoons gluten-free millet flour
1 tablespoon potato starch
2 tablespoons vanilla JELL-O® pudding powder

NOTE
If you see a fierce peachilla coming at you, run as quickly as you can in the opposite direction! Or not.

DIRECTIONS
Prepare your microwavable mug by coating the inside lightly with PAM Original cooking spray.

Mix the ingredients in a small bowl. Beat egg first with a spoon and mix in other liquid ingredients. Then add dry ingredients and mix until you've removed all the lumps.

Pour the batter into the mug (do not fill more than halfway) and smooth the top with a spoon. Thump mug firmly on the tabletop six times to remove excess air bubbles. Place mug on top of a microwavable small plate or saucer.

Bake for 3 - 4 minutes. Check for doneness by inserting a toothpick in the middle of the microwave mug cake and removing the toothpick. If the toothpick is dry, the MMC is done.

Wait 2 minutes, then run a butter knife along the inside of the mug, and tip the cake onto a plate. Position the mug cake so that the slightly rounded surface is on top. Your microwave mug cake will now look like a slightly overgrown muffin.

FANCY STUFF
Frost the whole Peachilla Microwave Mug Cake with Duncan Hines® Creamy Home-Style Classic Vanilla Frosting, or split the MMC in half, and frost each half individually (in which case you'll end up with two separate MMCs — or you can reassemble the frosted halves to create a layered MMC). Decorate, if you wish, with sliced peaches.

Peanut Butter and Strawberry Microwave Mug Cake

INGREDIENTS
1 egg
2 tablespoons Skippy® peanut butter
3 tablespoons Yoplait® Strawberry yogurt
3 tablespoons soy milk
2 tablespoons oil
1/8 teaspoon McCormick® vanilla extract
1/4 teaspoon Argo® baking powder
1/2 teaspoon guar gum, xantham gum, or tapioca flour
1/2 teaspoon McCormick® ground cinnamon
4 tablespoons Domino® light brown sugar
4 tablespoons gluten-free quinoa flour
4 tablespoons gluten-free sorghum flour
2 tablespoons potato starch

NOTE
Are very small strawberries ever nicknamed "Peanut?"

DIRECTIONS
Prepare your microwavable mug by coating the inside lightly with PAM Original cooking spray.

Mix the ingredients in a small bowl. Beat egg first with a spoon and mix in other liquid ingredients. Then add dry ingredients and mix until you've removed all the lumps.

Pour the batter into the mug (do not fill more than halfway) and smooth the top with a spoon. Thump mug firmly on the tabletop six times to remove excess air bubbles. Place mug on top of a microwavable small plate or saucer.

Bake for 3 - 4 minutes. Check for doneness by inserting a toothpick in the middle of the microwave mug cake and removing the toothpick. If the toothpick is dry, the MMC is done.

Wait 2 minutes, then run a butter knife along the inside of the mug, and tip the cake onto a plate. Position the mug cake so that the slightly rounded surface is on top. Your microwave mug cake will now look like a slightly overgrown muffin.

FANCY STUFF
Frost the whole Peanut Butter and Strawberry Microwave Mug Cake with Yoplait® Strawberry yogurt or Duncan Hines® Creamy Home-Style Strawberry Cream Frosting, or split the MMC in half, and frost each half individually (in which case you'll end up with two separate MMCs — or you can reassemble the frosted halves to create a layered MMC). Decorate, if you wish, with sliced strawberries.

Peanut Butter Sorghum Microwave Mug Cake

INGREDIENTS
1 egg
2 tablespoons Skippy® peanut butter
3 tablespoons rice milk
2 tablespoons oil
1/8 teaspoon McCormick® vanilla extract
1/4 teaspoon Argo® baking powder
1/2 teaspoon guar gum, xantham gum, or tapioca flour
1 tablespoon sorghum syrup (pure sorghum)
1/2 teaspoon McCormick® ground cinnamon
4 tablespoons Domino® light brown sugar
4 tablespoons gluten-free quinoa flour
4 tablespoons gluten-free sorghum flour
2 tablespoons potato starch

NOTE

If they sold peanut butter sorghum pieces, some film aliens might never have wanted to phone home!

DIRECTIONS
Prepare your microwavable mug by coating the inside lightly with PAM Original cooking spray.

Mix the ingredients in a small bowl. Beat egg first with a spoon and mix in other liquid ingredients. Then add dry ingredients and mix until you've removed all the lumps.

Pour the batter into the mug (do not fill more than halfway) and smooth the top with a spoon. Thump mug firmly on the tabletop six times to remove excess air bubbles. Place mug on top of a microwavable small plate or saucer.

Bake for 3 - 4 minutes. Check for doneness by inserting a toothpick in the middle of the microwave mug cake and removing the toothpick. If the toothpick is dry, the MMC is done.

Wait 2 minutes, then run a butter knife along the inside of the mug, and tip the cake onto a plate. Position the mug cake so that the slightly rounded surface is on top. Your microwave mug cake will now look like a slightly overgrown muffin.

FANCY STUFF
Frost the whole Peanut Butter Sorghum Microwave Mug Cake with Duncan Hines® Creamy Home-Style Butter Cream Frosting, or split the MMC in half, and frost each half individually (in which case you'll end up with two separate MMCs — or you can reassemble the frosted halves to create a layered MMC). Decorate, if you wish, with peanuts.

Peanut Butterscotch Microwave Mug Cake

INGREDIENTS

1 egg
2 tablespoons Skippy® peanut butter
3 tablespoons Yoplait® French Vanilla yogurt
3 tablespoons milk
2 tablespoons oil
1/8 teaspoon McCormick® vanilla extract
1/4 teaspoon Argo® baking powder
1/2 teaspoon guar gum, xantham gum, or tapioca flour
1/2 teaspoon McCormick® ground cinnamon
4 tablespoons Domino® light brown sugar
4 tablespoons gluten-free sorghum flour
4 tablespoons gluten-free millet flour
1 tablespoon potato starch
2 tablespoons butterscotch JELL-O® pudding powder

NOTE
When people make butter out of peanuts, do cows feel relieved?

DIRECTIONS

Prepare your microwavable mug by coating the inside lightly with PAM Original cooking spray.

Mix the ingredients in a small bowl. Beat egg first with a spoon and mix in other liquid ingredients. Then add dry ingredients and mix until you've removed all the lumps.

Pour the batter into the mug (do not fill more than halfway) and smooth the top with a spoon. Thump mug firmly on the tabletop six times to remove excess air bubbles. Place mug on top of a microwavable small plate or saucer.

Bake for 3 - 4 minutes. Check for doneness by inserting a toothpick in the middle of the microwave mug cake and removing the toothpick. If the toothpick is dry, the MMC is done.

Wait 2 minutes, then run a butter knife along the inside of the mug, and tip the cake onto a plate. Position the mug cake so that the slightly rounded surface is on top. Your microwave mug cake will now look like a slightly overgrown muffin.

FANCY STUFF

Frost the whole Peanut Butterscotch Microwave Mug Cake with Duncan Hines® Creamy Home-Style Butter Cream Frosting, or split the MMC in half, and frost each half individually (in which case you'll end up with two separate MMCs — or you can reassemble the frosted halves to create a layered MMC). Decorate, if you wish, with peanuts.

Pearonut Microwave Mug Cake

INGREDIENTS

1 egg
2 tablespoons Beech-Nut® Pears baby food
2 tablespoons milk
2 tablespoons oil
1/8 teaspoon McCormick® vanilla extract
1/4 teaspoon Argo® baking powder
1/2 teaspoon guar gum, xantham gum, or tapioca flour
1/2 teaspoon McCormick® ground cinnamon
4 tablespoons Domino® light brown sugar
3 tablespoons gluten-free almond flour
4 tablespoons gluten-free all-purpose flour
1 tablespoon potato starch
2 tablespoons coconut JELL-O® pudding powder

NOTE
Imagine if a coconut joined a partridge in a pear tree. Just imagine.

DIRECTIONS

Prepare your microwavable mug by coating the inside lightly with cooking spray.

Mix the ingredients in a small bowl. Beat egg first with a spoon and mix in other liquid ingredients. Then add dry ingredients and mix until you've removed all the lumps.

Pour the batter into the mug (do not fill more than halfway) and smooth the top with a spoon. Thump mug firmly on the tabletop six times to remove excess air bubbles. Place mug on top of a microwavable small plate or saucer.

Bake for 3 - 4 minutes. Check for doneness by inserting a toothpick in the middle of the microwave mug cake and removing the toothpick. If the toothpick is dry, the MMC is done.

Wait 2 minutes, then run a butter knife along the inside of the mug, and tip the cake onto a plate. Position the mug cake so that the slightly rounded surface is on top. Your microwave mug cake will now look like a slightly overgrown muffin.

FANCY STUFF

Frost the whole Pearonut Microwave Mug Cake with Duncan Hines® Creamy Home-Style Classic Vanilla Frosting, or split the MMC in half, and frost each half individually (in which case you'll end up with two separate MMCs — or you can reassemble the frosted halves to create a layered MMC). Decorate, if you wish, with sliced pears.

Pearstachio Microwave Mug Cake

INGREDIENTS

1 egg
2 tablespoons Yoplait® Pear yogurt
5 tablespoons milk
2 tablespoons oil
1/8 teaspoon McCormick® vanilla extract
1/4 teaspoon Argo® baking powder
1/2 teaspoon guar gum, xantham gum, or tapioca flour
1/2 teaspoon McCormick® ground cinnamon
4 tablespoons Domino® light brown sugar
1 tablespoon gluten-free coconut flour
3 tablespoons gluten-free brown or white rice flour
4 tablespoons gluten-free sorghum flour
1 tablespoon potato starch
2 tablespoons pistachio JELL-O® pudding powder

NOTE
Isn't it fortunate that we don't have to shell a pear or peel a pistachio nut?

DIRECTIONS

Prepare your microwavable mug by coating the inside lightly with PAM Original cooking spray.

Mix the ingredients in a small bowl. Beat egg first with a spoon and mix in other liquid ingredients. Then add dry ingredients and mix until you've removed all the lumps.

Pour the batter into the mug (do not fill more than halfway) and smooth the top with a spoon. Thump mug firmly on the tabletop six times to remove excess air bubbles. Place mug on top of a microwavable small plate or saucer.

Bake for 3 - 4 minutes. Check for doneness by inserting a toothpick in the middle of the microwave mug cake and removing the toothpick. If the toothpick is dry, the MMC is done.

Wait 2 minutes, then run a butter knife along the inside of the mug, and tip the cake onto a plate. Position the mug cake so that the slightly rounded surface is on top. Your microwave mug cake will now look like a slightly overgrown muffin.

FANCY STUFF

Frost the whole Pearstachio Microwave Mug Cake with Yoplait® Pear yogurt or Duncan Hines® Creamy Home-Style Classic Vanilla Frosting, or split the MMC in half, and frost each half individually (in which case you'll end up with two separate MMCs — or you can reassemble the frosted halves to create a layered MMC). Decorate, if you wish, with sliced pears.

Piña Colada Microwave Mug Cake

INGREDIENTS

1 egg
5 tablespoons milk
3 tablespoons Yoplait® Piña Colada yogurt
2 tablespoons oil
1/8 teaspoon McCormick® vanilla extract
1/4 teaspoon Argo® baking powder
1/2 teaspoon guar gum, xantham gum, or tapioca flour
1/2 teaspoon McCormick® ground cinnamon
4 tablespoons Domino® light brown sugar
4 tablespoons gluten-free sorghum flour
4 tablespoons gluten-free soy flour
1 tablespoon potato starch
2 tablespoons coconut JELL-O® pudding powder
2 tablespoons shredded coconut

NOTE
Remember the old Piña Colada song? It wasn't nearly as good as a Piña Colada Microwave Mug Cake.

DIRECTIONS

Prepare your microwavable mug by coating the inside lightly with cooking spray.

Mix the ingredients in a small bowl. Beat egg first with a spoon and mix in other liquid ingredients. Then add dry ingredients and mix until you've removed all the lumps.

Pour the batter into the mug (do not fill more than halfway) and smooth the top with a spoon. Thump mug firmly on the tabletop six times to remove excess air bubbles. Place mug on top of a microwavable small plate or saucer.

Bake for 3 - 4 minutes. Check for doneness by inserting a toothpick in the middle of the microwave mug cake and removing the toothpick. If the toothpick is dry, the MMC is done.

Wait 2 minutes, then run a butter knife along the inside of the mug, and tip the cake onto a plate. Position the mug cake so that the slightly rounded surface is on top. Your microwave mug cake will now look like a slightly overgrown muffin.

FANCY STUFF

Frost the whole Piña Colada Microwave Mug Cake with Yoplait® Piña Colada yogurt, or split the MMC in half, and frost each half individually (in which case you'll end up with two separate MMCs — or you can reassemble the frosted halves to create a layered MMC). Decorate, if you wish, with shredded coconut.

Pineapple Coconut Microwave Mug Cake

INGREDIENTS
1 egg
2 tablespoons Yoplait® Pineapple yogurt
3 tablespoons soy milk
2 tablespoons oil
1/8 teaspoon McCormick® coconut extract
  (or McCormick® vanilla extract)
1/4 teaspoon Argo® baking powder
1/2 teaspoon guar gum, xantham gum, or tapioca flour
1/2 teaspoon McCormick® ground cinnamon
4 tablespoons Domino® light brown sugar
2 tablespoons gluten-free coconut flour
4 tablespoons gluten-free brown or white rice flour
2 tablespoons potato starch
2 tablespoons shredded coconut

NOTE
If coconuts and pineapples are really tropical fruits, then why don't you ever see them with a suntan?

DIRECTIONS
Prepare your microwavable mug by coating the inside lightly with PAM Original cooking spray.

Mix the ingredients in a small bowl. Beat egg first with a spoon and mix in other liquid ingredients. Then add dry ingredients and mix until you've removed all the lumps.

Pour the batter into the mug (do not fill more than halfway) and smooth the top with a spoon. Thump mug firmly on the tabletop six times to remove excess air bubbles. Place mug on top of a microwavable small plate or saucer.

Bake for 3 - 4 minutes. Check for doneness by inserting a toothpick in the middle of the microwave mug cake and removing the toothpick. If the toothpick is dry, the MMC is done.

Wait 2 minutes, then run a butter knife along the inside of the mug, and tip the cake onto a plate. Position the mug cake so that the slightly rounded surface is on top. Your microwave mug cake will now look like a slightly overgrown muffin.

FANCY STUFF
Frost the whole Pineapple Coconut Microwave Mug Cake with Yoplait® Pineapple yogurt or Duncan Hines® Creamy Home-Style Classic Vanilla Frosting, or split the MMC in half, and frost each half individually (in which case you'll end up with two separate MMCs — or you can reassemble the frosted halves to create a layered MMC). Decorate, if you wish, with shredded coconut.

Pineapple Pear Microwave Mug Cake

INGREDIENTS

1 egg
4 tablespoons Beech-Nut® Pears & Pineapple baby food
2 tablespoons Yoplait® Pineapple yogurt
1/8 teaspoon McCormick® vanilla extract
1/4 teaspoon Argo® baking powder
1/2 teaspoon guar gum, xantham gum, or tapioca flour
1/2 teaspoon McCormick® ground cinnamon
4 tablespoons Domino® light brown sugar
5 tablespoons gluten-free millet flour
3 tablespoons gluten-free almond flour
1 tablespoon potato starch

NOTE
Why can't all fruit get along as well as pineapples and pears do?

DIRECTIONS

Prepare your microwavable mug by coating the inside lightly with cooking spray.

Mix the ingredients in a small bowl. Beat egg first with a spoon and mix in other liquid ingredients. Then add dry ingredients and mix until you've removed all the lumps.

Pour the batter into the mug (do not fill more than halfway) and smooth the top with a spoon. Thump mug firmly on the tabletop six times to remove excess air bubbles. Place mug on top of a microwavable small plate or saucer.

Bake for 3 - 4 minutes. Check for doneness by inserting a toothpick in the middle of the microwave mug cake and removing the toothpick. If the toothpick is dry, the MMC is done.

Wait 2 minutes, then run a butter knife along the inside of the mug, and tip the cake onto a plate. Position the mug cake so that the slightly rounded surface is on top. Your microwave mug cake will now look like a slightly overgrown muffin.

FANCY STUFF

Frost the whole Pineapple Pear Microwave Mug Cake with Yoplait® Pineapple yogurt, or split the MMC in half, and frost each half individually (in which case you'll end up with two separate MMCs — or you can reassemble the frosted halves to create a layered MMC). Decorate, if you wish, with sliced or diced pineapples or pears.

Pumpkin Cheesecake Microwave Mug Cake

INGREDIENTS
1 egg
2 tablespoons canned pumpkin
2 tablespoons Yoplait® French
  Vanilla yogurt
1 tablespoon milk
2 tablespoons oil
1/8 teaspoon McCormick® vanilla extract
1/4 teaspoon Argo® baking powder
1/2 teaspoon guar gum, xantham gum, or tapioca flour
1/2 teaspoon McCormick® ground cinnamon
4 tablespoons Domino® light brown sugar
4 tablespoons gluten-free buckwheat flour
4 tablespoons gluten-free sorghum flour
1 tablespoon potato starch
2 tablespoons cheesecake JELL-O® pudding powder

NOTE
*When little cakes have their
pictures taken, do they say
"cheese," too?*

DIRECTIONS
Prepare your microwavable mug by coating the inside lightly with PAM Original cooking spray.

Mix the ingredients in a small bowl. Beat egg first with a spoon and mix in other liquid ingredients. Then add dry ingredients and mix until you've removed all the lumps.

Pour the batter into the mug (do not fill more than halfway) and smooth the top with a spoon. Thump mug firmly on the tabletop six times to remove excess air bubbles. Place mug on top of a microwavable small plate or saucer.

Bake for 3 - 4 minutes. Check for doneness by inserting a toothpick in the middle of the microwave mug cake and removing the toothpick. If the toothpick is dry, the MMC is done.

Wait 2 minutes, then run a butter knife along the inside of the mug, and tip the cake onto a plate. Position the mug cake so that the slightly rounded surface is on top. Your microwave mug cake will now look like a slightly overgrown muffin.

FANCY STUFF
Frost the whole Pumpkin Cheesecake Microwave Mug Cake with Duncan Hines® Creamy Home-Style Classic Vanilla Frosting, or split the MMC in half, and frost each half individually (in which case you'll end up with two separate MMCs — or you can reassemble the frosted halves to create a layered MMC). Decorate, if you wish, with your choice of sliced fruit or gluten-free candies.

Raspberry Lime Rickey Microwave Mug Cake

INGREDIENTS

1 egg
2 tablespoons Yoplait® Key Lime Pie yogurt
1 tablespoon milk
2 tablespoons oil
1/8 teaspoon McCormick® vanilla extract
1/4 teaspoon Argo® baking powder
1/2 teaspoon guar gum, xantham gum, or tapioca flour
1/2 teaspoon McCormick® ground cinnamon
4 tablespoons Domino® light brown sugar
5 tablespoons gluten-free millet flour
4 tablespoons gluten-free all-purpose flour
1 tablespoon potato starch
2 tablespoons raspberry JELL-O® gelatin powder

NOTE
Why do they always call it a "lime rickey" instead of, say, a "lime lucy?"

DIRECTIONS

Prepare your microwavable mug by coating the inside lightly with PAM Original cooking spray.

Mix the ingredients in a small bowl. Beat egg first with a spoon and mix in other liquid ingredients. Then add dry ingredients and mix until you've removed all the lumps.

Pour the batter into the mug (do not fill more than halfway) and smooth the top with a spoon. Thump mug firmly on the tabletop six times to remove excess air bubbles. Place mug on top of a microwavable small plate or saucer.

Bake for 3 - 4 minutes. Check for doneness by inserting a toothpick in the middle of the microwave mug cake and removing the toothpick. If the toothpick is dry, the MMC is done.

Wait 2 minutes, then run a butter knife along the inside of the mug, and tip the cake onto a plate. Position the mug cake so that the slightly rounded surface is on top. Your microwave mug cake will now look like a slightly overgrown muffin.

FANCY STUFF

Frost the whole Raspberry Lime Rickey Microwave Mug Cake with Yoplait® Key Lime Pie yogurt, or split the MMC in half, and frost each half individually (in which case you'll end up with two separate MMCs — or you can reassemble the frosted halves to create a layered MMC). Decorate, if you wish, with raspberries.

Raspearry Molasses Microwave Mug Cake

INGREDIENTS

1 egg

2 tablespoons Beech-Nut® Pears &
Raspberries baby food

1 tablespoon Grandma's® Original Molasses

3 tablespoons milk

2 tablespoons oil

1/8 teaspoon McCormick® vanilla extract

1/4 teaspoon Argo® baking powder

1/2 teaspoon guar gum, xantham gum, or tapioca flour

1/2 teaspoon McCormick® ground cinnamon

4 tablespoons Domino® light brown sugar

4 tablespoons gluten-free buckwheat flour

4 tablespoons gluten-free sorghum flour

2 tablespoons potato starch

NOTE
*Do raspberries ever wish they had
stems the way that pears do?*

DIRECTIONS

Prepare your microwavable mug by coating the inside lightly with PAM Original cooking spray.

Mix the ingredients in a small bowl. Beat egg first with a spoon and mix in other liquid ingredients. Then add dry ingredients and mix until you've removed all the lumps.

Pour the batter into the mug (do not fill more than halfway) and smooth the top with a spoon. Thump mug firmly on the tabletop six times to remove excess air bubbles. Place mug on top of a microwavable small plate or saucer.

Bake for 3 - 4 minutes. Check for doneness by inserting a toothpick in the middle of the microwave mug cake and removing the toothpick. If the toothpick is dry, the MMC is done.

Wait 2 minutes, then run a butter knife along the inside of the mug, and tip the cake onto a plate. Position the mug cake so that the slightly rounded surface is on top. Your microwave mug cake will now look like a slightly overgrown muffin.

FANCY STUFF

Frost the whole Raspearry Molasses Microwave Mug Cake with Duncan Hines® Creamy Home-Style Classic Vanilla Frosting, or split the MMC in half, and frost each half individually (in which case you'll end up with two separate MMCs — or you can reassemble the frosted halves to create a layered MMC). Decorate, if you wish, with raspberries or sliced pears.

Razzy Apple Microwave Mug Cake

INGREDIENTS

1 tablespoon apple cider vinegar
1 tablespoon flaxseed meal
  plus 2 tablespoons cold water
2 tablespoons Yoplait® Red Raspberry yogurt
3 tablespoons apple juice
2 tablespoons oil
1/8 teaspoon McCormick® vanilla extract
1/4 teaspoon Argo® baking powder
1/2 teaspoon guar gum, xantham gum, or tapioca flour
1/2 teaspoon McCormick® ground cinnamon
4 tablespoons Domino® light brown sugar
4 tablespoons gluten-free soy flour
4 tablespoons gluten-free sorghum flour
2 tablespoons potato starch

NOTE
If a raspberry gets sunburned, how can it tell?

DIRECTIONS

Prepare your microwavable mug by coating the inside lightly with PAM Original cooking spray.

Mix the ingredients in a small bowl. Add flaxseed meal to liquid ingredients and beat together. Then add dry ingredients and mix until you've removed all the lumps.

Pour the batter into the mug (do not fill more than halfway) and smooth the top with a spoon. Thump mug firmly on the tabletop six times to remove excess air bubbles. Place mug on top of a microwavable small plate or saucer.

Bake for 3 - 4 minutes. Check for doneness by inserting a toothpick in the middle of the microwave mug cake and removing the toothpick. If the toothpick is dry, the MMC is done.

Wait 2 minutes, then run a butter knife along the inside of the mug, and tip the cake onto a plate. Position the mug cake so that the slightly rounded surface is on top. Your microwave mug cake will now look like a slightly overgrown muffin.

FANCY STUFF

Frost the whole Razzy Apple Microwave Mug Cake with Yoplait® Red Raspberry yogurt or Duncan Hines® Creamy Home-Style Classic Vanilla Frosting, or split the MMC in half, and frost each half individually (in which case you'll end up with two separate MMCs — or you can reassemble the frosted halves to create a layered MMC). Decorate, if you wish, with sliced apples.

Rice Pudding Microwave Mug Cake

INGREDIENTS

1 egg
1 tablespoon Yoplait® French
   Vanilla yogurt
3 tablespoons rice milk
2 tablespoons oil
1/8 teaspoon McCormick® vanilla extract
1/4 teaspoon Argo® baking powder
1/2 teaspoon guar gum, xantham gum, or tapioca flour
1/2 teaspoon McCormick® ground cinnamon
4 tablespoons Domino® light brown sugar
4 tablespoons gluten-free brown or white rice flour
4 tablespoons gluten-free sorghum flour
2 tablespoons potato starch
1 tablespoon leftover prepared Minute® rice
1 tablespoon Sun-Maid® Natural Sun-Dried Raisins

NOTE
There was once a guy named Rice who played for the Boston Red Sox. This recipe has nothing to do with him.

DIRECTIONS

Prepare your microwavable mug by coating the inside lightly with PAM Original cooking spray.

Mix the ingredients in a small bowl. Beat egg first with a spoon and mix in other liquid ingredients. Then add dry ingredients and mix until you've removed all the lumps.

Pour the batter into the mug (do not fill more than halfway) and smooth the top with a spoon. Thump mug firmly on the tabletop six times to remove excess air bubbles. Place mug on top of a microwavable small plate or saucer.

Bake for 3 - 4 minutes. Check for doneness by inserting a toothpick in the middle of the microwave mug cake and removing the toothpick. If the toothpick is dry, the MMC is done.

Wait 2 minutes, then run a butter knife along the inside of the mug, and tip the cake onto a plate. Position the mug cake so that the slightly rounded surface is on top. Your microwave mug cake will now look like a slightly overgrown muffin.

FANCY STUFF

Frost the whole Rice Pudding Microwave Mug Cake with whipped cream, or split the MMC in half, and frost each half individually (in which case you'll end up with two separate MMCs — or you can reassemble the frosted halves to create a layered MMC). Decorate, if you wish, with Sun-Maid® Natural Sun-Dried Raisins.

Scott's Banilla Apple Chip Microwave Mug Cake

INGREDIENTS
1 egg
2 tablespoons Mott's® applesauce
2 tablespoons Yoplait® Banana
  Crème yogurt
1 tablespoon milk
2 tablespoons oil
1/8 teaspoon McCormick® vanilla extract
1/4 teaspoon Argo® baking powder
1/2 teaspoon guar gum, xantham gum, or tapioca flour
1/2 teaspoon McCormick® ground cinnamon
4 tablespoons Domino® light brown sugar
4 tablespoons gluten-free sorghum flour
4 tablespoons gluten-free millet flour
1 tablespoon potato starch
2 tablespoons vanilla JELL-O® pudding powder
2 tablespoons HERSHEY'S® semi-sweet chocolate chips

NOTE
See, Scott? We knew you'd be a fan of gluten-free microwave mug cakes as soon as we found exactly the right flavor for you!

DIRECTIONS
Prepare your microwavable mug by coating the inside lightly with PAM Original cooking spray.

Mix the ingredients in a small bowl. Beat egg first with a spoon and mix in other liquid ingredients. Then add dry ingredients and mix until you've removed all the lumps.

Pour the batter into the mug (do not fill more than halfway) and smooth the top with a spoon. Thump mug firmly on the tabletop six times to remove excess air bubbles. Place mug on top of a microwavable small plate or saucer.

Bake for 3 - 4 minutes. Check for doneness by inserting a toothpick in the middle of the microwave mug cake and removing the toothpick. If the toothpick is dry, the MMC is done.

Wait 2 minutes, then run a butter knife along the inside of the mug, and tip the cake onto a plate. Position the mug cake so that the slightly rounded surface is on top. Your microwave mug cake will now look like a slightly overgrown muffin.

FANCY STUFF
Frost the whole Scott's Banilla Apple Chip Microwave Mug Cake with Yoplait® Banana Crème yogurt or Duncan Hines® Creamy Home-Style Classic Vanilla Frosting, or split the MMC in half, and frost each half individually (in which case you'll end up with two separate MMCs — or you can reassemble the frosted halves to create a layered MMC). Decorate, if you wish, with HERSHEY'S® semi-sweet chocolate chips.

Squash and Molasses Microwave Mug Cake

INGREDIENTS
1 egg
2 tablespoons Beech-Nut® Squash
baby food
1 tablespoon Grandma's® Original Molasses
3 tablespoons soy milk
2 tablespoons oil
1/8 teaspoon McCormick® vanilla extract
1/4 teaspoon Argo® baking powder
1/2 teaspoon guar gum, xantham gum, or tapioca flour
1/2 teaspoon McCormick® ground ginger
1/4 teaspoon McCormick® ground cinnamon
pinch of McCormick® ground cloves
4 tablespoons Domino® light brown sugar
4 tablespoons gluten-free quinoa flour
4 tablespoons gluten-free sorghum flour
2 tablespoons potato starch

NOTE
Why did they name the game of squash after a vegetable?

DIRECTIONS
Prepare your microwavable mug by coating the inside lightly with PAM Original cooking spray.

Mix the ingredients in a small bowl. Beat egg first with a spoon and mix in other liquid ingredients. Then add dry ingredients and mix until you've removed all the lumps.

Pour the batter into the mug (do not fill more than halfway) and smooth the top with a spoon. Thump mug firmly on the tabletop six times to remove excess air bubbles. Place mug on top of a microwavable small plate or saucer.

Bake for 3 - 4 minutes. Check for doneness by inserting a toothpick in the middle of the microwave mug cake and removing the toothpick. If the toothpick is dry, the MMC is done.

Wait 2 minutes, then run a butter knife along the inside of the mug, and tip the cake onto a plate. Position the mug cake so that the slightly rounded surface is on top. Your microwave mug cake will now look like a slightly overgrown muffin.

FANCY STUFF
Frost the whole Squash and Molasses Microwave Mug Cake with Duncan Hines® Creamy Home-Style Butter Cream Frosting, or split the MMC in half, and frost each half individually (in which case you'll end up with two separate MMCs — or you can reassemble the frosted halves to create a layered MMC). Decorate, if you wish, with your choice of sliced fruit or gluten-free candies.

Strawbapple Microwave Mug Cake

INGREDIENTS

1 egg
2 tablespoons Yoplait® Strawberry yogurt
2 tablespoons apple juice
2 tablespoons oil
2 tablespoons sorghum syrup (pure sorghum)
1/8 teaspoon McCormick® vanilla extract
1/4 teaspoon Argo® baking powder
1/2 teaspoon guar gum, xantham gum, or tapioca flour
1/2 teaspoon McCormick® ground cinnamon
4 tablespoons gluten-free sorghum flour
4 tablespoons gluten-free all-purpose flour
2 tablespoons potato starch

NOTE

Is Strawbapple at all similar to Pig Latin?

DIRECTIONS

Prepare your microwavable mug by coating the inside lightly with PAM Original cooking spray.

Mix the ingredients in a small bowl. Beat egg first with a spoon and mix in other liquid ingredients. Then add dry ingredients and mix until you've removed all the lumps.

Pour the batter into the mug (do not fill more than halfway) and smooth the top with a spoon. Thump mug firmly on the tabletop six times to remove excess air bubbles. Place mug on top of a microwavable small plate or saucer.

Bake for 3 - 4 minutes. Check for doneness by inserting a toothpick in the middle of the microwave mug cake and removing the toothpick. If the toothpick is dry, the MMC is done.

Wait 2 minutes, then run a butter knife along the inside of the mug, and tip the cake onto a plate. Position the mug cake so that the slightly rounded surface is on top. Your microwave mug cake will now look like a slightly overgrown muffin.

FANCY STUFF

Frost the whole Strawbapple Microwave Mug Cake with sorghum syrup or Yoplait® Strawberry yogurt, or split the MMC in half, and frost each half individually (in which case you'll end up with two separate MMCs — or you can reassemble the frosted halves to create a layered MMC). Decorate, if you wish, with your choice of sliced fruit or gluten-free candies.

Strawberry Cheesecake Microwave Mug Cake

INGREDIENTS

1 egg

2 tablespoons Yoplait® Strawberry Cheesecake yogurt

3 tablespoons milk

2 tablespoons oil

1 tablespoon tapioca syrup

1/8 teaspoon McCormick® vanilla extract

1/4 teaspoon Argo® baking powder

1/2 teaspoon guar gum, xantham gum, or tapioca flour

1/2 teaspoon McCormick® ground cinnamon

4 tablespoons Domino® light brown sugar

4 tablespoons gluten-free brown or white rice flour

4 tablespoons gluten-free sorghum flour

1 tablespoon potato starch

2 tablespoons cheesecake JELL-O® pudding powder

NOTE
We wouldn't use this cheesecake to bait a mousetrap. Mice just don't deserve it (although mice are pretty cute).

DIRECTIONS

Prepare your microwavable mug by coating the inside lightly with PAM Original cooking spray.

Mix the ingredients in a small bowl. Beat egg first with a spoon and mix in other liquid ingredients. Then add dry ingredients and mix until you've removed all the lumps.

Pour the batter into the mug (do not fill more than halfway) and smooth the top with a spoon. Thump mug firmly on the tabletop six times to remove excess air bubbles. Place mug on top of a microwavable small plate or saucer.

Bake for 3 - 4 minutes. Check for doneness by inserting a toothpick in the middle of the microwave mug cake and removing the toothpick. If the toothpick is dry, the MMC is done.

Wait 2 minutes, then run a butter knife along the inside of the mug, and tip the cake onto a plate. Position the mug cake so that the slightly rounded surface is on top. Your microwave mug cake will now look like a slightly overgrown muffin.

FANCY STUFF

Frost the whole Strawberry Cheesecake Microwave Mug Cake with Yoplait® Strawberry Cheesecake yogurt or Duncan Hines® Creamy Home-Style Strawberry Cream Frosting, or split the MMC in half, and frost each half individually (in which case you'll end up with two separate MMCs — or you can reassemble the frosted halves to create a layered MMC). Decorate, if you wish, with strawberries.

Strawberry Muffin Microwave Mug Cake

INGREDIENTS
1 egg
2 tablespoons Yoplait® Strawberry yogurt
1 tablespoon milk
2 tablespoons oil
1/8 teaspoon McCormick® vanilla extract
1/4 teaspoon Argo® baking powder
1/2 teaspoon guar gum, xantham gum, or tapioca flour
1/2 teaspoon McCormick® ground cinnamon
4 tablespoons Domino® light brown sugar
4 tablespoons gluten-free sorghum flour
4 tablespoons gluten-free millet flour
1 tablespoon potato starch
2 tablespoons vanilla JELL-O® pudding powder

NOTE
If you call a cute strawberry a "muffin," do you think she gets offended?

DIRECTIONS
Prepare your microwavable mug by coating the inside lightly with PAM Original cooking spray.

Mix the ingredients in a small bowl. Beat egg first with a spoon and mix in other liquid ingredients. Then add dry ingredients and mix until you've removed all the lumps.

Pour the batter into the mug (do not fill more than halfway) and smooth the top with a spoon. Thump mug firmly on the tabletop six times to remove excess air bubbles. Place mug on top of a microwavable small plate or saucer.

Bake for 3 - 4 minutes. Check for doneness by inserting a toothpick in the middle of the microwave mug cake and removing the toothpick. If the toothpick is dry, the MMC is done.

Wait 2 minutes, then run a butter knife along the inside of the mug, and tip the cake onto a plate. Position the mug cake so that the slightly rounded surface is on top. Your microwave mug cake will now look like a slightly overgrown muffin.

FANCY STUFF
Frost the whole Strawberry Muffin Microwave Mug Cake with Yoplait® Strawberry yogurt or Duncan Hines® Creamy Home-Style Strawberry Cream Frosting, or split the MMC in half, and frost each half individually (in which case you'll end up with two separate MMCs — or you can reassemble the frosted halves to create a layered MMC). Decorate, if you wish, with sliced strawberries.

Strawberry Rice Microwave Mug Cake

INGREDIENTS

1 egg
2 tablespoon Yoplait® Strawberry yogurt
3 tablespoons rice milk
2 tablespoons oil
1/8 teaspoon McCormick® vanilla extract
1/4 teaspoon Argo® baking powder
1/2 teaspoon guar gum, xantham gum,
or tapioca flour
1/2 teaspoon McCormick® ground cinnamon
4 tablespoons Domino® light brown sugar
4 tablespoons gluten-free brown or white rice flour
4 tablespoons gluten-free all-purpose flour
2 tablespoons potato starch

NOTE
No, you can't grow strawberries in your microwave oven. But that's okay. You can grow them inside your yogurt container if you add some soil…and have a whole lot of luck.

DIRECTIONS

Prepare your microwavable mug by coating the inside lightly with cooking spray.

Mix the ingredients in a small bowl. Beat egg first with a spoon and mix in other liquid ingredients. Then add dry ingredients and mix until you've removed all the lumps.

Pour the batter into the mug (do not fill more than halfway) and smooth the top with a spoon. Thump mug firmly on the tabletop six times to remove excess air bubbles. Place mug on top of a microwavable small plate or saucer.

Bake for 3 - 4 minutes. Check for doneness by inserting a toothpick in the middle of the microwave mug cake and removing the toothpick. If the toothpick is dry, the MMC is done.

Wait 2 minutes, then run a butter knife along the inside of the mug, and tip the cake onto a plate. Position the mug cake so that the slightly rounded surface is on top. Your microwave mug cake will now look like a slightly overgrown muffin.

FANCY STUFF

Frost the whole Strawberry Rice Microwave Mug Cake with Duncan Hines® Creamy Home-Style Strawberry Cream Frosting, or split the MMC in half, and frost each half individually (in which case you'll end up with two separate MMCs — or you can reassemble the frosted halves to create a layered MMC). Decorate, if you wish, with strawberries.

Strawmango Microwave Mug Cake

INGREDIENTS

1 egg

4 tablespoons Beech-Nut® Mango baby food

3 tablespoons Yoplait® Strawberry Mango yogurt

1/8 teaspoon McCormick® vanilla extract

1/4 teaspoon Argo® baking powder

1/2 teaspoon guar gum, xantham gum, or tapioca flour

1/2 teaspoon McCormick® ground cinnamon

4 tablespoons Domino® light brown sugar

4 tablespoons gluten-free sorghum flour

4 tablespoons gluten-free soy flour

1 tablespoon potato starch

NOTE

Why is it that strawberries and mangos so rarely have an excuse to just sit down and talk with one another?

DIRECTIONS

Prepare your microwavable mug by coating the inside lightly with cooking spray.

Mix the ingredients in a small bowl. Beat egg first with a spoon and mix in other liquid ingredients. Then add dry ingredients and mix until you've removed all the lumps.

Pour the batter into the mug (do not fill more than halfway) and smooth the top with a spoon. Thump mug firmly on the tabletop six times to remove excess air bubbles. Place mug on top of a microwavable small plate or saucer.

Bake for 3 - 4 minutes. Check for doneness by inserting a toothpick in the middle of the microwave mug cake and removing the toothpick. If the toothpick is dry, the MMC is done.

Wait 2 minutes, then run a butter knife along the inside of the mug, and tip the cake onto a plate. Position the mug cake so that the slightly rounded surface is on top. Your microwave mug cake will now look like a slightly overgrown muffin.

FANCY STUFF

Frost the whole Strawmango Microwave Mug Cake with Yoplait® Strawberry Mango yogurt, or split the MMC in half, and frost each half individually (in which case you'll end up with two separate MMCs — or you can reassemble the frosted halves to create a layered MMC). Decorate, if you wish, with sliced strawberries or mangos.

Sweet Potato Microwave Mug Cake

INGREDIENTS

1 egg
2 tablespoons Beech-Nut® Sweet
 Potato baby food
2 tablespoons rice milk
2 tablespoons oil
1/8 teaspoon McCormick® vanilla extract
1/4 teaspoon Argo® baking powder
1/2 teaspoon guar gum, xantham gum, or tapioca flour
1/2 teaspoon McCormick® ground cinnamon
1/4 teaspoon McCormick® ground nutmeg
4 tablespoons Domino® light brown sugar
4 tablespoons gluten-free brown or white rice flour
4 tablespoons gluten-free all-purpose flour
2 tablespoons potato starch

NOTE

One potato, two potato, sweet potato, four. Does anyone else feel like watching some vintage TV shows right about now?

DIRECTIONS

Prepare your microwavable mug by coating the inside lightly with cooking spray.

Mix the ingredients in a small bowl. Beat egg first with a spoon and mix in other liquid ingredients. Then add dry ingredients and mix until you've removed all the lumps.

Pour the batter into the mug (do not fill more than halfway) and smooth the top with a spoon. Thump mug firmly on the tabletop six times to remove excess air bubbles. Place mug on top of a microwavable small plate or saucer.

Bake for 3 - 4 minutes. Check for doneness by inserting a toothpick in the middle of the microwave mug cake and removing the toothpick. If the toothpick is dry, the MMC is done.

Wait 2 minutes, then run a butter knife along the inside of the mug, and tip the cake onto a plate. Position the mug cake so that the slightly rounded surface is on top. Your microwave mug cake will now look like a slightly overgrown muffin.

FANCY STUFF

Frost the whole Sweet Potato Microwave Mug Cake with Duncan Hines® Creamy Home-Style Classic Vanilla Frosting, or split the MMC in half, and frost each half individually (in which case you'll end up with two separate MMCs — or you can reassemble the frosted halves to create a layered MMC). Decorate, if you wish, with Sun-Maid® Natural Sun-Dried Raisins.

Tapi-Cocoa Microwave Mug Cake

INGREDIENTS

1 egg
2 tablespoons Yoplait® French
  Vanilla yogurt
2 tablespoons orange juice
2 tablespoons oil
2 tablespoons tapioca syrup
1/8 teaspoon McCormick® vanilla extract
1/4 teaspoon Argo® baking powder
1/2 teaspoon guar gum, xantham gum, or tapioca flour
4 tablespoons gluten-free sorghum flour
4 tablespoons gluten-free all-purpose flour
2 tablespoons HERSHEY'S® cocoa powder

NOTE
If cocoa beans wore taps, would they have a recital?

DIRECTIONS

Prepare your microwavable mug by coating the inside lightly with PAM Original cooking spray.

Mix the ingredients in a small bowl. Beat egg first with a spoon and mix in other liquid ingredients. Then add dry ingredients and mix until you've removed all the lumps.

Pour the batter into the mug (do not fill more than halfway) and smooth the top with a spoon. Thump mug firmly on the tabletop six times to remove excess air bubbles. Place mug on top of a microwavable small plate or saucer.

Bake for 3 - 4 minutes. Check for doneness by inserting a toothpick in the middle of the microwave mug cake and removing the toothpick. If the toothpick is dry, the MMC is done.

Wait 2 minutes, then run a butter knife along the inside of the mug, and tip the cake onto a plate. Position the mug cake so that the slightly rounded surface is on top. Your microwave mug cake will now look like a slightly overgrown muffin.

FANCY STUFF

Frost the whole Tapi-Cocoa Microwave Mug Cake with tapioca syrup, or split the MMC in half, and frost each half individually (in which case you'll end up with two separate MMCs — or you can reassemble the frosted halves to create a layered MMC). Decorate, if you wish, with sliced fruit.

Tapioca Tundra Microwave Mug Cake

INGREDIENTS

1 egg
**2 tablespoons Beech-Nut® Chiquita®
  Bananas baby food**
2 tablespoons orange juice
2 tablespoons oil
2 tablespoons tapioca syrup
1/8 teaspoon McCormick® vanilla extract
1/4 teaspoon Argo® baking powder
1/2 teaspoon guar gum, xantham gum, or tapioca flour
1/2 teaspoon McCormick® ground cinnamon
4 tablespoons gluten-free sorghum flour
4 tablespoons gluten-free all-purpose flour
2 tablespoons potato starch

NOTE
Since tapioca comes from cassava, why isn't it called tassioca instead?

DIRECTIONS

Prepare your microwavable mug by coating the inside lightly with PAM Original cooking spray.

Mix the ingredients in a small bowl. Beat egg first with a spoon and mix in other liquid ingredients. Then add dry ingredients and mix until you've removed all the lumps.

Pour the batter into the mug (do not fill more than halfway) and smooth the top with a spoon. Thump mug firmly on the tabletop six times to remove excess air bubbles. Place mug on top of a microwavable small plate or saucer.

Bake for 3 - 4 minutes. Check for doneness by inserting a toothpick in the middle of the microwave mug cake and removing the toothpick. If the toothpick is dry, the MMC is done.

Wait 2 minutes, then run a butter knife along the inside of the mug, and tip the cake onto a plate. Position the mug cake so that the slightly rounded surface is on top. Your microwave mug cake will now look like a slightly overgrown muffin.

FANCY STUFF

Frost the whole Tapioca Tundra Microwave Mug Cake with tapioca syrup, or split the MMC in half, and frost each half individually (in which case you'll end up with two separate MMCs — or you can reassemble the frosted halves to create a layered MMC). Decorate, if you wish, with sliced bananas.

The Great Pumpkin Microwave Mug Cake

INGREDIENTS
1 egg
1 tablespoon canned pumpkin
1 tablespoon Grandma's®
  Original Molasses
2 tablespoons Yoplait® French Vanilla yogurt
2 tablespoons oil
1/8 teaspoon McCormick® vanilla extract
1/4 teaspoon Argo® baking powder
1/2 teaspoon guar gum, xantham gum, or tapioca flour
1/2 teaspoon McCormick® ground cinnamon
4 tablespoons Domino® light brown sugar
4 tablespoons gluten-free sorghum flour
4 tablespoons gluten-free brown or white rice flour
2 tablespoons potato starch

NOTE
On Halloween Night, the Great Pumpkin rises out of his microwave oven – and you can snack on him!

DIRECTIONS
Prepare your microwavable mug by coating the inside lightly with PAM Original cooking spray.

Mix the ingredients in a small bowl. Beat egg first with a spoon and mix in other liquid ingredients. Then add dry ingredients and mix until you've removed all the lumps.

Pour the batter into the mug (do not fill more than halfway) and smooth the top with a spoon. Thump mug firmly on the tabletop six times to remove excess air bubbles. Place mug on top of a microwavable small plate or saucer.

Bake for 3 - 4 minutes. Check for doneness by inserting a toothpick in the middle of the microwave mug cake and removing the toothpick. If the toothpick is dry, the MMC is done.

Wait 2 minutes, then run a butter knife along the inside of the mug, and tip the cake onto a plate. Position the mug cake so that the slightly rounded surface is on top. Your microwave mug cake will now look like a slightly overgrown muffin.

FANCY STUFF
Frost the whole The Great Pumpkin Microwave Mug Cake with whipped cream, or split the MMC in half, and frost each half individually (in which case you'll end up with two separate MMCs — or you can reassemble the frosted halves to create a layered MMC). Sprinkle, if you wish, with McCormick® ground cinnamon.

Triple Coconut Microwave Mug Cake

INGREDIENTS
1 egg
2 tablespoons Yoplait® French Vanilla
  yogurt
3 tablespoons rice milk
2 tablespoons oil
1/8 teaspoon McCormick® coconut extract
  (or McCormick® vanilla extract)
1/4 teaspoon Argo® baking powder
1/2 teaspoon guar gum, xantham gum, or tapioca flour
1/2 teaspoon McCormick® ground cinnamon
4 tablespoons Domino® light brown sugar
2 tablespoons gluten-free coconut flour
4 tablespoons gluten-free all-purpose flour
1 tablespoon potato starch
2 tablespoons coconut JELL-O® pudding powder
2 tablespoons shredded coconut

NOTE
Ever wish you had three coconuts so you could juggle them? Well, the Triple Coconut Microwave Mug Cake is almost as good – if you know how to juggle.

DIRECTIONS
Prepare your microwavable mug by coating the inside lightly with PAM Original cooking spray.

Mix the ingredients in a small bowl. Beat egg first with a spoon and mix in other liquid ingredients. Then add dry ingredients and mix until you've removed all the lumps.

Pour the batter into the mug (do not fill more than halfway) and smooth the top with a spoon. Thump mug firmly on the tabletop six times to remove excess air bubbles. Place mug on top of a microwavable small plate or saucer.

Bake for 3 - 4 minutes. Check for doneness by inserting a toothpick in the middle of the microwave mug cake and removing the toothpick. If the toothpick is dry, the MMC is done.

Wait 2 minutes, then run a butter knife along the inside of the mug, and tip the cake onto a plate. Position the mug cake so that the slightly rounded surface is on top. Your microwave mug cake will now look like a slightly overgrown muffin.

FANCY STUFF
Frost the whole Triple Coconut Microwave Mug Cake with Duncan Hines® Creamy Home-Style Classic Vanilla Frosting, or split the MMC in half, and frost each half individually (in which case you'll end up with two separate MMCs — or you can reassemble the frosted halves to create a layered MMC). Decorate, if you wish, with shredded coconut.

Tutti Frutti Microwave Mug Cake

INGREDIENTS

1 egg
2 tablespoons Beech-Nut® Pears &
    Pineapple baby food
3 tablespoons apple juice
2 tablespoons oil
1/8 teaspoon McCormick® vanilla extract
1/4 teaspoon Argo® baking powder
1/2 teaspoon guar gum, xantham gum, or tapioca flour
1/2 teaspoon McCormick® ground ginger
1/4 teaspoon McCormick® ground cinnamon
pinch of McCormick® ground cloves
4 tablespoons Domino® light brown sugar
4 tablespoons gluten-free all-purpose flour
4 tablespoons gluten-free sorghum flour
2 tablespoons potato starch
2 tablespoons Sun-Maid® Natural Sun-Dried Raisins

NOTE
Wasn't Tutti Frutti one of the characters from the 1970s television show, "The Facts of Life?" No, never mind. That was Tootie.

DIRECTIONS

Prepare your microwavable mug by coating the inside lightly with PAM Original cooking spray.

Mix the ingredients in a small bowl. Beat egg first with a spoon and mix in other liquid ingredients. Then add dry ingredients and mix until you've removed all the lumps.

Pour the batter into the mug (do not fill more than halfway) and smooth the top with a spoon. Thump mug firmly on the tabletop six times to remove excess air bubbles. Place mug on top of a microwavable small plate or saucer.

Bake for 3 - 4 minutes. Check for doneness by inserting a toothpick in the middle of the microwave mug cake and removing the toothpick. If the toothpick is dry, the MMC is done.

Wait 2 minutes, then run a butter knife along the inside of the mug, and tip the cake onto a plate. Position the mug cake so that the slightly rounded surface is on top. Your microwave mug cake will now look like a slightly overgrown muffin

FANCY STUFF

Frost the whole Tutti Frutti Microwave Mug Cake with Duncan Hines® Creamy Home-Style Butter Cream Frosting, or split the MMC in half, and frost each half individually (in which case you'll end up with two separate MMCs — or you can reassemble the frosted halves to create a layered MMC). Decorate, if you wish, with Sun-Maid® Natural Sun-Dried Raisins.

Vanilla Boysenberry Microwave Mug Cake

INGREDIENTS

1 egg
2 tablespoons Yoplait® Boysenberry yogurt
4 tablespoons milk
2 tablespoons oil
1/8 teaspoon McCormick® vanilla extract
1/4 teaspoon Argo® baking powder
1/2 teaspoon guar gum, xantham gum, or tapioca flour
1/2 teaspoon McCormick® ground cinnamon
4 tablespoons Domino® light brown sugar
4 tablespoons gluten-free fava bean flour
4 tablespoons gluten-free all-purpose flour
1 tablespoon potato starch
2 tablespoons vanilla JELL-O® pudding powder

NOTE
We wonder whether somewhere, right now, some enterprising farmer is developing a girlsenberry.

DIRECTIONS

Prepare your microwavable mug by coating the inside lightly with PAM Original cooking spray.

Mix the ingredients in a small bowl. Beat egg first with a spoon and mix in other liquid ingredients. Then add dry ingredients and mix until you've removed all the lumps.

Pour the batter into the mug (do not fill more than halfway) and smooth the top with a spoon. Thump mug firmly on the tabletop six times to remove excess air bubbles. Place mug on top of a microwavable small plate or saucer.

Bake for 3 - 4 minutes. Check for doneness by inserting a toothpick in the middle of the microwave mug cake and removing the toothpick. If the toothpick is dry, the MMC is done.

Wait 2 minutes, then run a butter knife along the inside of the mug, and tip the cake onto a plate. Position the mug cake so that the slightly rounded surface is on top. Your microwave mug cake will now look like a slightly overgrown muffin.

FANCY STUFF

Frost the whole Vanilla Boysenberry Microwave Mug Cake with Yoplait® Boysenberry yogurt, or split the MMC in half, and frost each half individually (in which case you'll end up with two separate MMCs — or you can reassemble the frosted halves to create a layered MMC). Decorate, if you wish, with your choice of sliced fruit or gluten-free candies.

Vanilla Carrot Microwave Mug Cake

INGREDIENTS
1 egg
2 tablespoons Beech-Nut® Tender
  Sweet Carrots baby food
4 tablespoons milk
2 tablespoons oil
1/8 teaspoon McCormick® vanilla extract
1/4 teaspoon Argo® baking powder
1/2 teaspoon guar gum, xantham gum, or tapioca flour
1/2 teaspoon McCormick® ground cinnamon
4 tablespoons Domino® light brown sugar
4 tablespoons gluten-free fava bean flour
4 tablespoons gluten-free brown or white rice flour
1 tablespoon potato starch
2 tablespoons vanilla JELL-O® pudding powder

NOTE
It's pretty hard to find vanilla carrots growing in the wild because, every time bunnies find a clump, they dig them up and eat them.

DIRECTIONS
Prepare your microwavable mug by coating the inside lightly with PAM Original cooking spray.

Mix the ingredients in a small bowl. Beat egg first with a spoon and mix in other liquid ingredients. Then add dry ingredients and mix until you've removed all the lumps.

Pour the batter into the mug (do not fill more than halfway) and smooth the top with a spoon. Thump mug firmly on the tabletop six times to remove excess air bubbles. Place mug on top of a microwavable small plate or saucer.

Bake for 3 - 4 minutes. Check for doneness by inserting a toothpick in the middle of the microwave mug cake and removing the toothpick. If the toothpick is dry, the MMC is done.

Wait 2 minutes, then run a butter knife along the inside of the mug, and tip the cake onto a plate. Position the mug cake so that the slightly rounded surface is on top. Your microwave mug cake will now look like a slightly overgrown muffin.

FANCY STUFF
Frost the whole Vanilla Carrot Microwave Mug Cake with Duncan Hines® Creamy Home-Style Classic Cream Cheese Frosting, or split the MMC in half, and frost each half individually (in which case you'll end up with two separate MMCs — or you can reassemble the frosted halves to create a layered MMC). Decorate, if you wish, with Sun-Maid® Natural Sun-Dried Raisins.

Very Cherry Microwave Mug Cake

INGREDIENTS

1 egg
4 tablespoons Beech-Nut® Apples & Cherries baby food
3 tablespoons Yoplait® Cherry Orchard yogurt
1/8 teaspoon McCormick® vanilla extract
1/4 teaspoon Argo® baking powder
1/2 teaspoon guar gum, xantham gum, or tapioca flour
1/2 teaspoon McCormick® ground cinnamon
4 tablespoons Domino® light brown sugar
4 tablespoons gluten-free sorghum flour
4 tablespoons gluten-free soy flour
1 tablespoon potato starch

NOTE
How cherry, exactly, is very cherry?

DIRECTIONS

Prepare your microwavable mug by coating the inside lightly with cooking spray.

Mix the ingredients in a small bowl. Beat egg first with a spoon and mix in other liquid ingredients. Then add dry ingredients and mix until you've removed all the lumps.

Pour the batter into the mug (do not fill more than halfway) and smooth the top with a spoon. Thump mug firmly on the tabletop six times to remove excess air bubbles. Place mug on top of a microwavable small plate or saucer.

Bake for 3 - 4 minutes. Check for doneness by inserting a toothpick in the middle of the microwave mug cake and removing the toothpick. If the toothpick is dry, the MMC is done.

Wait 2 minutes, then run a butter knife along the inside of the mug, and tip the cake onto a plate. Position the mug cake so that the slightly rounded surface is on top. Your microwave mug cake will now look like a slightly overgrown muffin.

FANCY STUFF

Frost the whole Very Cherry Microwave Mug Cake with Yoplait® Cherry Orchard yogurt, or split the MMC in half, and frost each half individually (in which case you'll end up with two separate MMCs — or you can reassemble the frosted halves to create a layered MMC). Decorate, if you wish, with sliced cherries.

INDEX

NO ADDED DAIRY

NO ADDED EGGS

Chocolate Chip Orange Microwave Mug Cake 25
Chocolateberry Microwave Mug Cake 30
Coconut Peach Microwave Mug Cake 35
Lemony Microwave Mug Cake 59
Razzy Apple Microwave Mug Cake 84

NO ADDED SUGAR

Appleach Microwave Mug Cake 5
Blueberry Malted Microwave Mug Cake 16
Chocolate Chip Sorghum Microwave Mug Cake 26
Coffee Sorghum Microwave Mug Cake 39
Corn Appleberry Microwave Mug Cake 40
Corny Raisin Microwave Mug Cake 42
Molasses Pudding Microwave Mug Cake 64
Peach Sorghum Microwave Mug Cake 71
Strawbapple Microwave Mug Cake 88
Tapi-Cocoa Microwave Mug Cake 94
Tapioca Tundra Microwave Mug Cake 95

NO ADDED OIL

Appearcot Microwave Mug Cake 2
Apple Coffee Microwave Mug Cake 4
Banana Soy Microwave Mug Cake 13
Butterscotch Coffee Microwave Mug Cake 18
Chocolate-Covered Carrot Microwave Mug Cake 31
Chocopeach Molasses Microwave Mug Cake 33
Fruit Medley Microwave Mug Cake 46
Fruits 'n Nuts Microwave Mug Cake 48
Pineapple Pear Microwave Mug Cake 80
Strawmango Microwave Mug Cake 92
Very Cherry Microwave Mug Cake 101

RESOURCES

If you're on a gluten-free diet, or you know someone who is, you have plenty of company – finally. Gluten-free eating is becoming increasingly popular. Some people choose gluten-free diets for heath reasons and, in fact, they may be under doctor's orders to avoid gluten. Others choose gluten-free eating because they believe – and, in some cases, they know – that it makes them feel better.

Bakeries, coffee shops, restaurants, and supermarkets are accommodating gluten-free eaters – but the change isn't happening quickly enough to make gluten-free baking items everyday products. It still takes some legwork to find such "exotic" gluten-free baking products as gluten-free flours, guar gum, xantham gum, and potato starch. To order these specialized gluten-free products, try these resources:

Bob's Red Mill
13521 SE Pheasant Court
Milwaukie, Oregon 97222
Customer Service: (800) 349-2173
www.bobsredmill.com

Arrowhead Mills
Consumer Relations
The Hain Celestial Group, Inc.
4600 Sleepytime Dr.
Boulder, CO 80301
Customer Service: (800) 434-4246
www.arrowheadmills.com

Barry Farm Foods
20086 Mudsock Road
Wapakoneta, OH 45895
Customer Service (419) 741-0155
www.barryfarm.com

Vitacost.com
Customer Service (800) 381-0759
www.vitacost.com

Other brand name products that we cite in our recipes may be easier to find in some supermarkets, depending upon where you live. But it's always wise to check on the product's current gluten-free status (or to check with your doctor) before you commit to buying the product. Therefore (and also because your local supermarket might not have the particular brands we mention, and you might want to buy them online or locate another store that stocks the brands), here are the corporate web sites for the brand name products we've mentioned in the recipes:

McCormick® extracts and spices
Customer Service (800) 632-5847
www.mccormick.com

Domino® light brown sugar
Customer Service (800) 729-4840
www.dominosugar.com

Argo® baking powder
Customer Service (866) 373-2300
www.argostarch.com/index.html

Yoplait® Original yogurt
Customer Service (800) 967-5248
www.yoplait.com

JELL-O® pudding powder and gelatin powder
Customer Service (877) 535-5666
brands.kraftfoods.com/jello

Minute® rice
Customer Service (800) 646-8831
www.minuterice.com

Skippy® peanut butter
Customer Service (866) 475-4779
www.peanutbutter.com

HERSHEY'S® semi-sweet chocolate chips and cocoa powder
Customer Service (800) 468-1714
www.hersheys.com

Grandma's® Original Molasses
Customer Service available only online at
www.bgfoods.com/about/contact.asp
www.bgfoods.com/grandmas/grandmas_products.asp

Duncan Hines® frostings
Customer Service (800) 362-9834
www.duncanhines.com/products/frostings

Beech-Nut® baby foods
Customer Service (800-233-2468)
www.beechnut.com

Sun-Maid® Natural Sun-Dried Raisins
Customer Service (559-896-8000)
www.sunmaid.com

We'd love your feedback.
Please visit www.microwavemugcakes.com and become
part of the Microwave Mug Cake community!

CPSIA information can be obtained at www.ICGtesting.com
Printed in the USA
LVOW111616200212

269551LV00001B/79/P